Formal Theory in Sociology

SUNY Series, The New Inequalitites

A. Gary Dworkin, Editor

Formal Theory in Sociology

Opportunity or Pitfall?

edited by
Jerald Hage

State University of New York Press

Published by
State University of New York Press, Albany

Printed in the United States of America

For information, address the State University of New York Press,
State University Plaza, Albany, NY 12246
Production by Christine Lynch
Marketing by Theresa Abad Swierzowski

Library of Congress Cataloging-in-Publication Data

Formal theory in sociology : opportunity or pitfall? / edited by
    Jerald Hage.
        p.   cm. — (SUNY series, the new inequalities)
    Includes bibliographical references and index.
    ISBN 0-7914-1951-7 (acid-free). — ISBN 0-7914-1952-5 (pbk. : acid
-free)
    1. Sociology—Methodology.   2. Sociology—Philosophy.   I. Hage,
Jerald, 1932- .   II. Series.
    HM24.F672   1994
    301'.01—dc20   93-32114
                                                                 CIP

10 9 8 7 6 5 4 3 2 1

Contents

List of Tables

List of Figures

Introduction

Without doubt, the topic of theory in sociology and the need for a formalization of existing theories today are of the utmost significance for the discipline.

During the late 1960s and early 1970s, a number of books (Willer 1967; Stinchcombe 1968; Dubin 1969; Blalock 1969; Reynolds 1971; Gibbs 1972; Hage 1972) pleaded for more formal theory and in some instances attempted to indicate how formal theories could be constructed. Yet, this surprisingly strong surge of interest in formal theory died adorning as it were. By the middle of the 1970s, although a few more books appeared (most notably Chavetz 1978), concern for formal theory had largely died and graduate courses on the topic disappeared.

For scholars interested in the sociology of knowledge this rapid birth and death of an intellectual movement poses a number of questions. Why did such a widely based effort fail so quickly and decisively? Certainly, the authors involved were not minor figures in the field. Many of them were located at the most visible universities and several subsequently became officers of the American Sociological Association. Therefore, their visibility is not in question. Nor is the reason that inherently the subject matter of sociology prevents the development of formal theory convincing, because economics has clearly continued to emphasize formal theory and did not suffer from the attacks against positivism that emerged during the 1970s (see the Collins contribution in part 1). We should, therefore, look elsewhere for an explanation to the demise of this short-lived effort.

With this thought in mind, I applied to the American Sociological Association to organize a conference on the causes for the "death" of formal theory. With a generous grant from the Association and institutional support from the University of Maryland, a conference was held at the University of Maryland in August of 1990, just before the annual meetings. Significantly, the conference took place almost two decades or a "generation" after the publication of these books on theory construction that were cited previously.

1

A major motivating idea behind the conference was that, by understanding why this movement had failed, we might be able to provide insights into how to renew interest in formal theory. Certainly, I hoped that we would develop recommendations about necessary changes in the nature of graduate education in sociology, a topic that is discussed in part 3. Even more directly, participants were asked to consider the following but related question: Have the circumstances that prevailed in the late 1960s and early 1970s changed enough so that a similar effort might be more successful? History teaches but only those who are willing to reflect upon the past and discover the mistakes that were made so as not to repeat them.

WHY CHOOSE TO HAVE A CONFERENCE ABOUT FORMAL THEORY NOW?

After two decades of reflecting upon the fact that my own theory construction book did not have as much impact as I hoped, it occurred to me that others who have also attempted to influence the nature and the direction of the discipline probably had, like me, reflected a great deal about this issue. Failure frequently teaches more than success!

I also felt that twenty years is a long enough time to give someone distance about one's work. Certainly, in hindsight if I were to rewrite my own book on theory construction, there would be considerable changes in what was emphasized (chapter 9). The field has changed, of course, and any book on formal theory would inevitably reflect these changes. Furthermore, I can now more easily perceive errors in my own reasoning. It seemed reasonable to assume that this would be true for the other participants as well. A conference in the mid-seventies would have been likely to produce an ideological response upon the part of those who were interested in formal theory. Hopefully, time and intellectual distance gained through additional experiences generates wisdom. The reader will have to judge for himself or herself whether I waited long enough for such wisdom to emerge.

But even more fundamentally, I have been concerned over the past decade, specifically from the beginning of the Reagan attacks on social science in general and sociology in particular, about the vulnerability of sociology to criticisms about its intellectual merit. For years, sociology has been viewed as the weak sister in the social sciences, especially when compared to economics and psychology, and even to political science. Whether one uses indicators such as enrollment demand at both the undergraduate and graduate levels, number of employment positions in industry or government, funding by the National Science Foundation or other relevant funding sources, academic salaries, and so forth, it is readily apparent to all that sociology is not in a powerful position. Therefore, I felt that a conference about formal theory was useful in the light of ten years of continued cuts in funding for sociology.

Consistent with signs of weakness, other, stronger disciplines have begun to absorb or solve many of the problems that were once the sole concern of sociologists, as Collins and Waller mention in the first part of this book. Specifically economics is attempting to analyze a number of issues that are important to sociology, including the family, the sociology of education, and organizational sociology. Conversely, some of the new perspectives in sociology are merely economic paradigms thinly disguised: rational choice theory, governance theory, and even population-ecology theory, while also having biological roots, are all based on the primordial concern for efficiency. Cognitive psychology is similarly encroaching upon social psychology, threatening many of the job opportunities that would otherwise be available for our PhDs.

Confirming my concerns about the intellectual invasion from stronger disciplines, I saw the closing of the sociology department at Washington University as an ominous sign. Admittedly many issues were involved in this decision but the closing enjoyed wide publicity and received considerable support in the general community. Since the conference held in 1990, we have observed the struggles to retain sociology at San Diego and most critically Yale university. And while the latter was a success story, the fact still remains that in many universities serious doubts about the utility of sociology endure. As the funding of higher education becomes more and more precarious—and it will be during the 1990s—universities will cut those departments that they believe are less central to their mission. The University of Maryland has already done so and closed seven departments. Fields perceived as weak will be the first ones to be endangered. So a second and hardly minor reason for holding a formal theory conference now was the relevance of formal theory for the status and survival of the discipline. Admittedly, strengthening formal theory is not the only answer to critiques of the discipline, but it is one that speaks directly to the issue of the intellectual merit of the field.

The concerns that I have just outlined were shared by the participants in our conference. While not all contributors to this book agree about whether formal theory should be used in sociology, they do agree that research projects must articulate with the development of theories in specific subfields so that the discipline accumulates knowledge. Furthermore, some of this knowledge should be relevant to the real world if the discipline is to gain power, prestige and most critically prepare its practitioners for nonteaching positions. These positions only emerge when people believe that sociologists have worthwhile insights that are not obvious and that relate to at least some practical concerns. This does not mean that sociology should become applied but with predictive theory sociologists will be hired to analyze social issues.

Still a third reason for the conference flows from the previous one. The attacks on sociology as a discipline have had precisely the kinds of effects that Simmel would have predicted. There is now much greater cohesion in the field. But even without these attacks on the discipline there have been a number of changes in the past twenty years that make a reconsideration of the pros and cons of formal theory a timely exercise. The Vietnam War is not only over but the country appears to have come to terms with it. Parallelly, the politicization and paradigmatic conflict that have characterized sociology has largely damped (Ritzer 1990). The generation who completed their graduate degrees in the 1960s are now in control of most sociology departments; they have become the power structure and therefore the problem of power for them appears less central.

Reflecting this change in zeitgeist, synthetic articles are now more and more common in the journals. It is not unusual nowadays to read, in the inevitable review of the literature, a discussion of several different paradigms. Furthermore, most of the articles are written by several authors, indicating that teamwork is becoming the norm, amounting to an amazing change. One major advantage of multiple authorship is that it allows for the kind of methodological sophistication that Blalock asks for (chapter 7), combined with a serious consideration of theory.

Generational swings occur in intellectual interests as well as in the economy, as Wiley (1990) has suggested. Not unexpectedly, several articles about the state of sociology have appeared by some of the contributors to this conference (Collins and Blalock), calling for a return to the idea of sociology as a science. There are new articles appearing in theory construction (Walker and Cohen 1985) that also reflect a renewed interest in formal theory. Pawson (1988) has proposed a new approach, a realist perspective, that bridges a number of differences in the old debate about positivism. Hage and Meeker (1988) have done the same in the area of social causality, suggesting an ontological paradigm that is more appropriate for the social sciences.

But perhaps the best signs of synthesis and collaboration are to be found in the new debates within theory itself. The discussions of agency and structure, and micro and macro reflect attempts to combine the disparate branches of the discipline and encourage people to work on issues that bring together different kinds of epistemological and ontological assumptions. The theory section of the American Sociological Association now alternates in its selection of officers to reflect a much wider vision of what is important in the field. In short, all of these signs indicated that a conference on formal theory might be useful.

THE CHOICE OF THE PARTICIPANTS

Seusing that many of the individuals who were originally involved might have reflected upon the reasons why *their* particular contributions did not make a dent on the consciousness of the sociological fraternity and sorority, I invited a number of them to share their views. Specifically, Blalock, Chafetz, Cohen, Davies, and Gibbs—all of whom have written formal theory construction books—were invited to attend. Because of a prior commitment, James Davies was unable to participate. In addition, Peter Abell, who has written the only book on theory construction published in England, was invited to participate in order to provide a different perspective.

However, restricting the conference to original participants could lead to distortion. Therefore, a general appeal was advertised in *Perspectives*, the theory section newsletter. Unfortunately no one responded. Given this, several scholars—Jonathan Turner, Randall Collins, and Gerhard Lenski (again, he was the only one who could not attend)—who have written about theory and from different perspectives, were invited to analyze the same set of issues. In addition, two discussants, with quite divergent views about the wisdom of formal theory—Stephen Turner and David Willer—were asked to comment about the papers that were prepared.

THE ORGANIZATION OF THE PAPERS.

As anyone who has organized a conference knows, one can ask people to write papers about certain themes or topics but what emerges is not necessarily congruent with the plans. Although I had detailed conversations about themes of the conference, the authors proceeded to move in new directions that were of interest of them. This does not mean that the papers were scattered. On the contrary, all of the participants mentioned how pleased they were about attending a conference that had such focus and where all the papers were reasonably on target. Rarely are conferences as specific in topic as this one was, and the result is the remarkable coherence of the papers collected in this book. Given this strong focus, the arrangement of the papers became somewhat arbitrary. They have been organized into two parts, but many of the topics in part 2 contain ideas relevant to the theme of part 1 and vice-versa. As a consequence, I have written extended introductions to each part so that the reader can skip back and forth depending upon the topic that is of interest.

The basic question of the conference—why did the theory construction movement die so quickly—is the theme of part 1. Besides presenting a wide diversity of reasons, these papers present a most interesting debate. The first three (Collins and Waller, Turner, and Hage) argue that a scientific approach to sociology has not been taken seriously within the discipline and for a wide variety of causes, while the fourth chapter (Cohen) suggests that this is too global and sweeping a judgment, and that there are some areas where formal theory has thrived and continues to grow. Thus, one issue is whether or not the influence of formal theory did wane completely. Particularly interesting is the fact that Cohen is the one who has most recently written a book on formal theory construction, one that has been successful enough to be reprinted.

But not surprisingly a new and unanticipated topic emerged from the papers. The second part centers more directly on this emergent theme: What is formal theory? It is one thing to argue that the remedy for providing substance to the discipline is formal theory and quite another to agree upon what formal theory is. Thus, the nature of formal theory becomes an important issue for debate in the second part (although, again, ideas on this topic appear in the first part as well). One of the most interesting points being made is that the meaning of formal theory has largely shifted in the past twenty years from the emphasis on hypotheses to more deductive modes of reasoning and certainly much more complex theoretical models.

Finally, the contributions in this book represent the considered opinions of individuals who have thought about these matters over a very long time. As a consequence there is an intellectual density to them that makes this collection of papers quite unusual. It was clear that the conference could have easily spent several days debating these issues—plus others—and that there was not enough time in a single-day conference to have a full hearing of all of the issues. But it is our hope that these papers will encourage others to think and reflect about formal theory and its relevance for the power and status of the discipline.

Part I
The Demise of Theory Construction

The relatively sudden appearance of so many books on theory construction during the five years of 1968–1972 represents a unique experience in the history of sociology. Seldom have there been so many contributions and so much apparent consensus on the need for material and yet within only a few years such a total lack of interest at least as evidenced by the absence of any new articles or books on the topic. Usually new specialties grow slowly, gradually gaining adherents. Furthermore, many of the leading sociology departments added theory construction courses to their graduate programs and then abandoned them within a few years. It would appear that the topic of formal theory was in the same class as hula hoops; a fashion that almost explodes and just as quickly disappears.

The first three papers in this first part provide a large array of reasons for this sudden demise. The first two contributions include three authors, Collins and Waller, and Turner, who did *not* write books about theory construction and in fact have grave doubts about the utility of attempting to find techniques that will help people to think. Given their original skepticism, their analysis is especially interesting. Their analysis is contrasted with two other authors, Hage and Cohen, who have each published a book on formal theory.

In chapter 1 and 2, Collins and Waller and Turner provide a good overview of the historical context in which the theory construction books appeared. A case history of one particular area, feminist scholarship, is provided in chapter 8 by Chafetz, who indicates that the feminists have rejected the idea of "panhistorical and cross-cultural generalizations."

Collins and Waller attempt to place the arguments about positivism in sociology in a comparative disciplinary context, observing that some disciplines, including some in the social sciences such as economics and psychology, were not touched by the debate that has continued in sociology. Their general explanation is that disciplines with a strong and expanding academic base, which is related to expansion in nonacademic jobs as well, gradually invade those disciplines that do not have the same opportunities. The most fascinating argument that they make is that fields are not inherently "hard" or "soft" but instead it depends upon their theoretical strategies and thus by implication their definition of formal theory. If so, then the idea of changing the nature of the relative importance of formal theory in sociology, the focus of part 2, has enormous implications.

The impact of an antipositivist mood also hit English sociology as Abell observes in chapter 6. But he argues that there was an enormous increase in the number of academic positions for sociology, with both the large interest in the social sciences and the humanities and the creation of a large number of new universities and polytechniques, but given the period when they received their training, they were imprinted with a view of theory not unlike that of Giddens (1984), who has forcibly maintained that formal theory is a waste of effort. Presumedly, the same circumstance occurred in the United States; a large number of students finished their graduate training precisely when formal theory came under attack. As Abell observes, these are the people who control the positions of power in the discipline—and in both countries—so that prospects for formal theory are limited indeed. But now that almost twenty-five years has passed, there may be a new generation moving to occupy these same positions, providing another opportunity for a new debate about the appropriateness of formal theory.

Gibbs in chapter 5 in part 2 traces another consequence of the antipositivist swing, a loss of interest in predictive theory. He suggests that one of the barriers to the development of theory has been that the grandfathers of sociology used the discursive mode so that this form of theorizing has enormous legitimacy. It becomes difficult to argue against the theory format of Marx, Weber, Durkheim, and Simmel (and others) because it implies that one is arguing against the theory. Thus, in accepting the message one also accepts the medium. In contrast, the feminists rejected both the grandfathers and formal theory (see chapter 8) even though they were not formalists.[1]

If Collins and Waller provide a broad and interesting comparative sweep across the entire range of academic disciplines, Turner in chapter 2 gives us a long historical view of the way in which the work in sociology has been organized. His general observation is that sociology has never had enough power to control its agenda and particularly to prevent other disciplines or the public from believing that they can practice sociology just as well as any of our PhDs. One of his themes, and one that emerges in many of the other papers, is the fragmentation that occurs as a consequence of lack of control over the agenda of the discipline. This theme of fragmentation is particularly central to the analysis in the Hage paper (chapter 3), while the separation between theory and methodology is lamented by Blalock (chapter 7). Abell (chapter 6) describes the same condition, when he suggests that in England theory and empirical research have been disconnected and this has prevented the accumulation of knowledge. Likewise Chafetz (chapter 8) observes the same problem in feminist scholarship.

Turner in chapter 2 emphasizes the lack of cognitive standardization through formal theory as being the natural outcome of the lack of power and the resulting fragmentation, while Hage in chapter 3 suggests that these tendencies emerge given the original intellectual starting points of the discipline. Obviously, which position one takes implies quite different solutions to the problem. In Turner's view, as is apparent in his figure, there is no exit from the vicious cycle and there would never appear to be a solution for increasing the worth of the discipline. We are compelled to remain in a marginal status.

Finally, Hage in his contribution in this part, comments that the timing of the theory books could not have been worse. The discontent with American society and more specifically American involvement in the Vietnam War resulted in a different kind of recruitment into sociology precisely as antipositivism emerged (which is cause and which is effect?). Together, these events politicized sociology departments more than has occurred in most of the other social sciences, resulting in a loss of creditability with academic administrators, state legislators, and even the general public. Nor were these the only sources of discontent. Both gender and racial inequality were also (and perhaps still) are keenly felt. Given the recruitment patterns into sociology because of its central concern with stratification and therefore inequality, greater politicization and distrust of the past—and thus attempts at formal theory—was inevitable.

In part agreeing with Turner about the power of the discipline, Hage suggests a potential solution in his analysis of why formal theory did not succeed by arguing that the complex reality of sociology with its more difficult measurement problems requires a collective effort, one that has not been made. Some examples of group efforts in building formal theory are given in the Cohen chapter. But these issues of what to do about changing the marginal status of sociology are the subject of the third and concluding part.

One of the more interesting sections of Turner's analysis is the futility of the theory construction movement—its inappropriate understanding of what is theory, its naive belief in the possibility of a methodology of theory construction, and its choice of the wrong scientific discipline, physics, as a model. Thus, Turner presents the case that theory construction contributed to its own demise by advocating the wrong view of how formal theory should be constructed and what should be constructed, that is the choice of the physics model of formal theory. What is arresting about this line of reasoning is that it is epistemological, quite unlike the more general theme of disciplinary powerless in the rest of the Turner's contribution and of the Collins and Waller piece as well. However, the Turner analysis of the theory construction movement implies much more unity in perspective than was true. His critique about the hopes for a methodology of theory construction can only be usefully applied to those by Hage and Blalock and while many of the books did emphasize axiomatic theory it was presented as only one of a variety of viewpoints. Hage in chapter 3 suggests that the more distinctive characteristics of the texts is their quite disparate views of what is theory construction and formal theory, another example of fragmentation even within subspecialties of the discipline!

Quite a separate epistemological and ontological argument is presented in the beginning of chapter 3, where Hage contends that the social reality confronting sociologists requires formal theories, which are inherently more complicated to construct and that simultaneously pose also more severe methodological and statistical obstacles. Thus, one can agree with the feminists who disavow panhistorical and cross-cultural generalizations and others who take a narrow positivist approach that ignores differences in gender, race, and other kinds of social categories. But scope conditions speak directly to this problem as they add much more complexity to our theoretical formulations. Furthermore, scope conditions can be applied across historical time as Hage illustrates in chapter 9. This theme about the complex methodological issues is the substance of Blalock's paper (chapter 7), where he argues that theorists have ignored empirical data and the complex reasoning that is involved. Thus, while agreeing with Turner about the history of sociology, Hage is suggesting that it was not just a question of power but also of an essential starting point in the nature of sociological reality, an origin that as Turner observes involved taking those intellectual problems that were left over from the disciplines of economics, psychology, and political science. Hage places more emphasis on the quite distinctive intellectual strategies and interests of the founding fathers, which prevents a common perspective.[2]

Equally important in Hage's view is that specialization was combined with politicization. Collins and Waller also observe that sociology has had a large number of debates although they emphasis the battleground between positivist and antipositivist tendencies. Chafetz (chapter 8) observes a parallel distrust of attempts at generalization. Perhaps the right critique but the wrong solution—avoidance of formal theory is not necessarily the best or the only possibility.

Collins and Waller locate one source of this politicization in the field's not having a secure academic basis, while Hage argues that there has been a particular pattern of recruitment related to the subject matter of the discipline that exacerbated the politicization process during the Vietnam War.

The impact of politicization on the choice of strategies relative to theory building and its consequences for views about formal theory are explicated in chapter 8 where Chafetz discusses how feminists came to reject formal theory. This becomes almost a case history of how sociology became politicized. Many of the arguments against formal theory employed by the feminists resonated with others who felt that the power structure had to be destroyed and formal theory was seen as part of the problem of domination, as Abell indicates in his discuss of the Continental influences on sociological theory.

Turner suggests that one of the major losses associated with the demise of the theory construction movement was the loss of interest in formal theory, a position with which Gibbs (chapter 5) would agree. In contrast, several examples of where formal theory have been continuously pursued are suggested in Cohen's paper. And in the Collins and Waller piece several others are noted as well. But while there are exceptions including Turner's own work, it may be difficult to characterize the sociological cup as half full. But then an overall characterization by anyone is almost impossible since we are limited by own expertise and reading. Perhaps it is time that the discipline actually attempt an inventory of what areas formal theory has been developed in?

Notes

1. The interesting exception is, of course, Marx, who was very much interested in formal theory and most consciously was concerned about his basic assumptions and their deductions.

2. For example, much of Weber's work while agreeing with many of the ideas contained in Marx is suggesting that there are enormous exceptions of values and bureaucracies. The work of Simmel and Durkheim is equally distinctive when contrasted with each other and, of course, the divergence between their subject matter and explanations and those of Marx and Weber could not be greater. The four also illustrate quite divergent styles of formal theory and strategies for constructing theory.

1

Did Social Science Break Down in the 1970s?

Randall Collins and David Waller

The movement for systematic explanatory theories in sociology was afoot by the 1950s and gathered momentum through the 1970s. There have been a variety of styles; the most important of these has been the effort to state substantive theories in a series of causal or correlational propositions, and to systematically relate these to each other and to bodies of evidence. This style appeared thirty years ago in organizational theory, most explicitly in Hage's axiomatic theory (1965), also giving a formal backbone to March and Simon (1958) and Thompson (1967). There was some of this propositional style in developing conflict theory, including Coser (1956), Dahrendorf (1959), Lenski (1966), and Collins' (1975) effort to provide a summary of propositions and cross-validate them by sketching their mutual coherence. Exchange theory did not have this formalizing style in early works of Homans and Blau, but reached it with Emerson (1972); it has been prominent in the program of expectation states theory (Berger et al. 1974, 1983) as well as Willer's Elementary Theory (Willer and Anderson 1981; Willer 1987).

Most of these lines of work have continued in recent years, and some have extended the formal style. Jonathan Turner's (1984) formal theory of stratification pulls together the strands of the conflict theories; Cook (1982), Jasso (1988), and others extended the themes of exchange theory and connected it to network theory; exchange theory broadened into rational choice theory by importing full-scale mathematical techniques from economics, which have been carried furthest in Coleman's recent work (1990). New systematic micro-theories have appeared, such as Heise's affect-control-chains (1979) and Kemper's (1978) social interactional theory of emotions; the healthiness of both theories a decade later in shown in Kemper (1990).

Why then should we talk about a crisis in formal theory? Part of the problem is an internal parting of the Ways, a series of disagreements over where the emphasis should lie. Should one concentrate on establishing a methodology of formal theory construction, or proceed from the substantive side and find one's way pragmatically toward formal theory via successive approximations? How closely should theory construction be tied to empirical data: should it be tied to operationalization and statistical test from the outset (the Gibbs strategy, 1989)? Or to a program of laboratory experiments (the EST, exchange-network and Willer ET strategies—the last of which rejects statistical methodology)? Or can it use qualitative observational and historical data (my own preference—Collins 1984)? Why not build formal theory independently of the data, leaving the latter for experimentalists, thus paralleling the division of labor in physics (the Jon Turner strategy, 1988)? We have a further issue of the language in which the theory is to be expressed, ranging from verbal propositions to all-out mathematization, with various intermediate positions possible, including flow-chart models and computer simulations.

Yet another range of internal disagreements has to do with the substantive content of theories. This is not surprising considering that formal theories have been proposed within research traditions as different as conflict theory, organizational theory, ecological, evolutionary, and sociobiological theories, utilitarian theories on one side and affectual and moral theories on the other, cognitive and anticognitive models, micro and macro theories.

It seems obvious that we are not going to settle these problems soon. One might say these are healthy problems of a science with a subject matter as complex as human social life. We do have some of the pieces of the puzzle, thus far more often captured in verbal rather than highly formal statements. If this were purely an internal matter for people interested in building a scientific sociology, we could have confidence that gradually we will resolve our differences in style and substance. We could expect new lines of disagreement to emerge as older ones get settled, but that is just what happens at the research frontier of a science.

What gives us a sense of crisis is that some of our colleagues now tell us that the whole project of creating a sociological science is wrong. We are told rather vociferously that it is impossible, out-of-date, or immoral; that it is authoritarian, politically reactionary, racist, and antifeminist. Not all of these accusations are made at once, but these are components of a broad antipositivist front which has grown up in the last two decades. We will not discuss the substance of these criticisms here; they range from technical points of philosophy and methodology, to the crudest level of ideological polemic. What we will attempt to do is to use the methods of the sociology of science to show why an antipositivist movement became strong in wide areas of the academic world since the 1970s. In some fields it has become almost the reigning orthodoxy, in others it is one of the factions in a metatheoretical civil war.

The fact that antipositivist movements emerged in some fields more strongly than in others gives us some leverage in looking for their causes. In what follows we will sketch the places where antipositivist movements have hardly appeared at all (mathematics and the natural sciences generally; within the social sciences, economics, linguistics, psychology, artificial intelligence); the places which have become antipositivist strongholds (literary criticism, anthropology, to some extent history); and fields which have been battlegrounds between proscientific and antipositivist approaches (philosophy, political science, sociology, and in its own way, fine arts). Structural changes in the organization of the academic world in the 1970s, especially the expansion and then contraction of enrollments, hit these disciplines in different ways. We will suggest how the degree of crisis in the material underpinnings of disciplines produced hybrid movements flowing across disciplinary boundaries and challenging older intellectual identities. These movements have come from both sides of the field; there have been hyperpositivist imperialisms (such as sociobiology and rational choice) as well as antipositivisms crossing the borders. There is a general structural upheaval underlying all of these particular movements. The framework of the argument is set forth in table 1.1.

Our argument here is no more than a tentative sketch. A great deal of work would be needed to document the career crises which hit various disciplines. Moreover, our analysis of these patterns is based largely on the United States. Fortunately, Bourdieu's *Homo Academicus* (1984/1988) gives a detailed picture of the French intellectual field where so much of the antipositivist upheaval started. A more satisfactory analysis than our attempt would have to look at the flow of antipositivist movements in relation to the fortunes of academic fields in Britain, Europe, and the rest of the world.

FIELDS IMMUNE TO ANTIPOSITIVIST MOVEMENTS

There are a range of positions which might be called ''antipositivist.'' From the mildest to the most extreme these include: (1) Rejection of a particular philosophical program, especially the Vienna Circle's logical positivism in its most extreme formulations such as those of Carnap and Ayer; one might also reject milder versions such as Popper's falsification doctrine. (2) Rejection of formal or quantitative methods. (3) Rejection of the possibility of any generalized knowledge—the alternatives are to endorse localized, historically or culturally particularistic knowledge—or skepticism about any knowledge whatsoever. (4) Rejection of science as a political or moral evil.

TABLE 1.1
Positivist and Antipositivist Movements in U.S. Academic Fields

	Academic Market	Research Conditions	Paradigm Shift
Fields Immune to Antipositivist Movements			
Mathematics & Physical Sciences			
Biological Sciences*	expanding		"age of biology"
Economics *	steady growth		
Psychology	boom		cognitive revolution psychobiology
Linguistics *	growth		generative grammar
Artificial Intelligence*	boom		new field
Antipositivist Strongholds			
Literature	boom & bust	exhaustion of classical texts	literary theory, deconstruction
History	boom & bust	exhaustion of materials	cultural history, deconstruction
Anthropology	growth and decline	disappearance of tribal societies	symbolic anthropology
Battlegrounds			
Political Science	boom & decline		rational choice, historicism
Sociology	boom & bust		sociobiology, rational choice, historicism, culturology
Philosophy	mild fluctuation		postpositivism, "death of philosophy"; rationality & AI debates
Fine Arts		museum boom	postmodernist theory vs. traditional scholarship

* = paradigm-exporting field.

Mathematics and Natural Science.

Mathematics and the natural sciences have virtually no antipositivist movements in any of these senses. "Logical positivism" in the narrower sense was a movement of philosophers, not of practicing scientists; the faults that have been found with logical positivism typically have had no repercussions in natural science one way or the other. There have been some long-standing issues about the limits of formal consistency in mathematics and of determinacy in physics; but neither mathematical intuitionists nor quantum indeterminists have rejected either formality or generality. The recent development of chaos theory is misinterpreted by antipositivist outsiders; chaos theory is itself a mathematical model of regions of determinacy and indeterminacy. The nearest thing to an antipositivist theory within natural science is Prigogine's scheme of irreversible, nonequilibrium sequences in the emergence of physical and chemical structures; this has been seized upon as supporting historical particularism and holism in the social sciences (Wallerstein 1983), but it does not seem to be regarded as contrary to normal science within its own field.

Some scientists have been politically active in attacking applications of science involving military weapons, ecological and medical dangers. Though this sometimes meshes with the more general "science is dangerous" ideology, most activist scientists take the stance that their own scientific expertise is valid and should be put to use in public controversies. Scientific activists are rarely antipositivists. Geology, where one might have expected that the ideological fervor of the environmentalist movement would penetrate, nevertheless has seen an expansion of formal scientific models. This imperviousness to outside ideologies is related to the fact that geology has undergone a growth spurt since mid-century, with major leaps forward in formal theorizing based on new depth instrumentation and the mapping of the ocean floor.

Some natural scientists have aggressively exported their ideas into other intellectual fields. This is especially true of the biological sciences, which have gone through massive expansion in funding and personnel since World War II. The molecular biology revolution was itself the result of migration of physicists and chemists into the "soft" areas of biology. With the burgeoning of medical and commercial applications, these sciences have been riding a wave of confidence. One result has been imperialist movements such as sociobiology and population genetics, which have penetrated "softer" targets in the social sciences. In sociology, the most successful of these has been population ecology of organizations; sociobiology has faced strong resistance, in part because of its difficulty in dealing with short-term variations, and in part because of our long-standing political opposition to racism and our cultural capital invested in a social level of explanation.

IMMUNITIES TO ANTIPOSITIVISM WITHIN THE SOCIAL SCIENCES

Economics.

The social science which has stayed most closely on the positivist course has been economics. It was never much concerned with the philosophy of logical positivism, perhaps because economic theory has been largely deductive. Ever since the marginalist revolution of the 1870s, economics has been dominated by mathematical methods of theory construction; with the development of econometrics since the 1920s, its data side has been formalized as well. That is not to say that economics has been generally successful with all of its explanatory problems; questions of social distribution and of macrodynamics have not made much progress, and some experts have questioned whether the neoclassical apparatus is capable of handling these problems. Nevertheless, economics has had virtually no antipositivist challenge in the 1960s or later. There has been a long-standing rival approach, institutional economics, which goes back to the German historical economics of the nineteenth century; but this has had no notable upsurge during the recent period, nor has it attracted attention by intellectual breakthroughs of its own.[1]

Neither the intellectual shortcomings of neoclassical economics nor charges of conservative political bias generated a substantial antipositivist movement. Marxist economics surged with the left-wing student movement and even achieved a degree of institutionalization; but Marxist economists typically use formal methods and sources of data that do not depart greatly from the positivist mold (if avoiding ultra refinements of mathematical theory). Analytical Marxism in the form developed by Elster (1985) and Roemer (1986) goes in the other direction, bringing Marxist techniques up to date by reformulations using the approaches of game theory and rational actors.

Economics has been one of the idea-exporting disciplines since the 1970s. Rational choice models have expanded not only into the traditional problems of sociology but also of political science, law, and public policy. In philosophies like Rawls', it even penetrates the turf of philosophy.

Linguistics.

Linguistics during this period went through the Chomskyian revolution. What it replaced, Bloomfieldian linguistics, was a positivistic behaviorism. But although Chomskyian linguistics overthrew the emphasis on empirical induction, replacing it with analysis of the linguist's own intuitions, the result was not antipositivism. Instead, Chomskyian generative grammar opened a new terrain for formal analysis. Rival schools that have since emerged are all formal. They have been bolstered by alliance with the new fields of computer science and artificial intelligence.

Why linguistics in the United States (and some other places) went in this direction is a puzzle. In contrast, the tradition of linguistics in France (deriving from Saussure's structuralism, the Russian formalists of the 1920s, and the Prague school) was a main inspiration for the movement of semiotics which became a central component of the antipositivist front.

Psychology.

Psychology has been transformed by two sweeping movements since the 1960s. The so-called "cognitive revolution" displaced the once-dominant behaviorism. And clinical psychology expanded enormously since clinical degrees began to be offered separately from experimental psychology programs. One might have expected both of these movements to be adjuncts to the larger antipositivist wave of the times, but this was so to a much lesser degree than one might suppose.

During the heyday or behaviorism, the most famous cognitive psychology, Piaget's developmental scheme, was regarded as unscientifically soft and was largely confined to the French-speaking world. The cognitive revolution overthrew the narrow operationalism of the behaviorists. It threw off a restricted positivist methodology, and widened the terrain upon which science could operate to include the "black box" of the mind. In this respect anglophone psychology followed the same path as linguistics during its Chomskyian revolution, and was probably influenced by it. In both cases, computer modelling provided a basis for being "scientific" even without empirical data gathered by quantitative measurement.[2] The upsurge of artificial intelligence research has further bolstered the cognitivists, perhaps giving them dominance in academic psychology. It appears that the most hardline of the behaviorist factions, the Skinnerians, had the greatest staying power, while other forms of behaviorist learning theory have declined. Where psychology was once overwhelmingly environmentalist, one wing has gone in the direction of physiological processes, biochemical and genetic control of behavior. Part of psychology seems to have been absorbed by the imperialism of the biological sciences; but its antireductionist wing has also prospered, largely in alliance with computer modelling.

Clinical psychology might seem an exception to these patterns. In the late 1980s, the professional organization of U.S. psychologists split between a now minority of experimentalists and the new majority of clinicians. Clinical psychology in the 1960s and 1970s did have a humanistic and partially antipositivist tone; this was especially prominent in encounter groups, Gestalt therapy (a neo-Freudianism oriented towards cognitive and emotional exercises), and psychedelic and quasi-religious movements of activist therapy. It would appear though that the success of clinical psychology in expanding nonacademic careers is not based on an antipositivist stance. Among the most successful branches of clinical psychology have been behavior modification, an application of Skinnerian reinforcement schedules, now used in controlling smoking, school and child-development programs, and in criminology. Broadening the conception of rewards to include social reinforcement has brought a rapprochement between the behavior therapy and group-experience therapy practices.

Most of the expansion of clinical psychology has come by widening its clientele, away from medically-defined mental illness and towards "normal" problems. This has allowed psychologists to avoid a turf battle with medically licensed psychiatrists, while opening up large numbers of jobs. Within the mental illness area itself, the Freudian schools which were once prominent in psychiatric training now have largely given way to biological approaches. Genetic and physiological explanations and therapies (or projected therapies) have become prominent. One is reminded that the counterculture movement of the 1960s and 1970s, for all its ideology of antipositivism, was also the psychedelic drug movement, spearheaded by LSD. Itself the offshoot of biochemical laboratories, and led by break-away psychologists such as Leary, Alpert, and Groff, it is not surprising that the movement of participatory psychotherapy which it spawned should easily fall back into a more positivist version of drug therapy.

Artificial Intelligence.

Artificial intelligence (AI) is the other burgeoning new science in recent decades. Like Chomskyian linguistics and the new cognitive psychology, it thrives on materials that were formerly considered too "soft" for science. AI appears to have no connection with the philosophy and methodology of logical positivism. AI seems not to be greatly concerned with metatheoretical rules at all but is pressing ahead with its substantive work, inventing its method as it goes along. AI has taken as its research frontier problems such as recursiveness, reflexivity, fuzzy sets, and other issues which overflow the narrow confines of traditional positivism. It appears that with the exception of economics, the social sciences which have best survived the antipositivist challenge have been those which have thrown off Vienna Circle–style methodological restrictions while going on to build formal models around "softer" data.

ANTIPOSITIVIST STRONGHOLDS

Literature.

The center of antipositivism in the last decade has been departments of literature. The various overlapping movements called "New Literary Theory," semiotics, structuralism or post structuralism,[3] deconstructionism, and postmodernism have become very much in vogue, above all in the United States.

The origins of most of these movements are in French intellectual circles, dating back as far as the semiotic Freudianism of Lacan in the 1950s, and the culture criticism of Barthes and Derrida's combination of literature and philosophy in the 1960s. Postmodernism dates from the turn of the 1980s, and is connected to the repudiation of Marxism by radical French intellectuals at that time. It is in the 1970s and 1980s that these movements have become so prominent in American literature departments. We conjecture that because literature is the commonest academic base of editors in publishing houses, this kind of semiotic/antipositivist movement has been able to multiply its influence in other fields where scholars publish in books as much as in journal articles. This is one way in which the antipositivist ideology has spread into history and the social sciences.

These movements are more than a negative antipositivism. They can be regarded as ideologies glorifying literature. An epistemology which says in effect that the world is a text (or at least cannot be understood in any other way than as a reading of a text) makes literary criticism the queen of the sciences. Why did literature departments embrace this position so enthusiastically at just this time? We will confine our answer tot he anglophone academic world. The predominant literary method before 1960 was "New Criticism," introduced in the 1930s. New Criticism was something like a narrow positivism in the realm of literary methodology. It examined the techniques by which the author achieved effects, and rejected larger interpretations of meaning and historical significance. "New Literary Theory" was a kind of antipositivist revolution within the methods of literary criticism. It opened up just the issues of political, moral, and aesthetic significance that New Criticism had ruled out.

The theoretical/semiotic turn within literature can be regarded as a solution to a problem which was weighing ever more heavily on the careers of literature professors (Lamont 1987). Literature departments make their living by commenting on canonical literatures. But the number of classics does not grow very rapidly with the passing years (especially since the production of "classics" in the novel, epic poem, and drama seem to have ended by 1940). Literary critics have overworked their best material as time goes on, and were forced to specialize in increasingly obscure writings. New Criticism, by turning attention to method rather than substance, opened up one new turf for the professors, but it turned criticism inwards onto technicalities and cut them off from the lay audience of intellectuals to which literature had traditionally appealed. The New Literary Theory gave literature back its broader intellectual audience, and also gave it claims to a leading place throughout history and the social sciences as well.

This movement in literary criticism is somewhat ambiguous in the larger politics of the intellectual world. If the career problem of literature professors was to overcome the narrow esoteric specialities into which they had been driven, any theoretical imports would be welcome which gave literature a wider significance and connected it to themes in the surrounding intellectual world. New Literary Theory expands from textual analysis to the social world which produced texts and the readership which interprets them. It is latently ambiguous as to whether it is antipositivist or not. In one direction its themes are hyper-relativist, contextual, a version of the conundrums of philosophical skepticism. In another direction, it invites sociological explanations onto its turf and flirts with the more deterministic aspects of linguistics. So far its sociology has been largely confined within the assumption of Marxian culture-critique; but as Marxian ideology loses its prestige (a development which seems inevitable near the end of the twentieth century), literature itself may become a battleground between more sociological/explanatory and antipositivist approaches.

Anthropology.

In the social sciences, the antipositivist center is anthropology. Strictly speaking, one should say the center is social and cultural anthropology; archeology, physical anthropology, and anthropological linguistics remain oriented to measurement and description, often using the hardware of the natural sciences.

The antipositivist takeover of cultural and social anthropology has been building up for some time. There was an earlier school of diffusionists, dating back to the beginnings of the professional discipline around the time of Boas, which battled the contemporary positivism of evolutionists and racialists. Functionalism became prominent in anthropology in the 1920s (slightly earlier than it did in sociology), and antipositivism was in part a countermovement throwing off functionalism in the 1960s, much as a similar countermovement in sociology at the time. Marxist anthropology was part of this same movement, at least one wing of which, Marvin Harris' cultural materialism, is in some respects rather positivist; while the Marxism of Sahlins moved increasingly to the antipositivist side. Geertz's "thick description" is closest to the global antipositivist movement, combining the particularism of specialized field studies with the claim for some broader resonance in the realm of systems of meaning.

Anthropology is another field with a crisis in its source of cultural capital. The raw materials of classic anthropology have been dying out with the commercialization and political incorporation of the globe. Anthropologists have had the choice of becoming historical comparativists; moving their field research to modern settings; or finding some new way to define their distinctive approach. The first two alternatives meant that anthropologists were becoming some other kind of social scientists (comparative sociologists, development economists, urbanologists). A version of semiotic/ antipositivism gave them a chance to maintain their disciplinary identity, and to ally with a wider movement that valued particularism, relativism, and an anti-Western viewpoint.

History.

History does not seem to harbor as much militant antipositivism as literature and anthropology, but it has had an upsurge of this approach. It is not surprising that historians would find appeal in an ideology which declares that only particular configurations exist, and that these can never be definitively interpreted but only reinterpreted from a series of shifting standpoints. This is in effect the old historicist philosophy espoused by Dilthey against the claims of nineteenth-century positivism; the new version adds a constructivist twist that promises there will always be work for scholars to do, since every interpretation can always be deconstructed. Historians have some of the same problems of exhausting their cultural capital as literary critics do. Modern historical events add new materials more slowly than the rate at which historical scholars turn out research articles, and the prestige of historical studies is always oriented towards the great problems of the past where the competition is greatest.

Historians have been on the outlook for new realms to study or new methods to use on traditional topics. The study of cultural phenomena, at the hands of a Foucault or a Darnton, expands what a historian can do. But such studies risk becoming exercises in esoteric minutiae if they are not framed by a metatheory which gives them wider significance. Here again we see the ambivalence of the semiotic style. It is overtly antipositivist, but is also makes a generalizing appeal by claiming to uncover structures of mentality or of culture which have very wide significance. At the same time, other historians have been expanding into what is in effect sociological history or economic history using technical tools. History is another soft target for outside frames and methods. The antipositivist program of cultural analysis fits best with the emphasis on particularistic description which has always defined the historian's turf; but it is in competition with social science styles as well.

ANTIPOSITIVIST BATTLEGROUNDS

Philosophy.

Anglophone philosophy a generation ago was a stronghold of logical positivism, but even then there were rival positions. From its outset in the late 1920s, Vienna Circle positivism was criticized as extreme and its antimetaphysical stance as self-contradictory. The Vienna Circle had many British and American admirers, and its members migrated to those countries in the Nazi period, never returning to Europe. But the dominant stance in anglophone philosophy during mid-century was a broader movement of analytical philosophy. One wing continued the logical positivist emphasis on formal logic, although limiting its reductionist empiricism; another wing focused on ordinary language, continuing the effort to dissolve metaphysical issues into clarifications of language, while contributing to the "linguistic turn" in the intellectual world generally. The logical positivists seem to have had their strongest external influence on U.S. social science, as it was Vienna Circle refugees with their pupils and allies (Hans Reichenbach, Ernest Nagel, Carl Hempel; in Britain, Karl Popper and his followers) who wrote many of the influential metatheoretical textbooks of the period.

Early in the twentieth century, positivist philosophy in Germany shared the field with Neo-Kantianism, phenomenology, and existentialism, all of which in one degree or another were unfavorable to the knowledge-claims of natural science. Hegelianism and other German positions were imported into France in the 1920s and 1930s, and developed by French existentialists, phenomenologists, and Marxists in the 1940s through the 1960s. The 1960s saw an upsurge of structuralism and structuralist Marxism, together with critiques such as Derrida's deconstructionism and Foucault's politics of discourse; at the end of the 1970s, postmodernism became the slogan for disillusioned intellectuals turning away from its previous icons, Marxism and Freudianism.

The most prestigeful antipositivist movements of the last two decades have been these recent French movements. Yet their antipositivism in not particularly new. In France and Germany (and most other countries influenced by them), philosophy has not had a strong movement of positivist or analytical philosophy since the days of the Vienna Circle. The main exceptions in Germany have been some followers of Popper, plus some importing of ordinary language philosophy of Habermas and Apel. Most philosophy in France since Bergson at the beginning of the century has been critical of science. The main exception were Lévi-Straussian structuralism and Althusserian structuralist Marxism, which claimed to be unlocking, respectively, the structural code of the human mind or of the systems of social and economic organization. Deconstructionist and postmodernist movements pointedly rejected these scientific pretentions; thus the later twist in French antipositivism is to some extent an internal turf battle against the popular positions just preceding. When such ideas have been imported into the United States, the broadly structuralist phase (Lévi-Strauss, Foucault, Althusser) has been amalgamated with the antistructuralists (Derrida, Lyotard, Baudrillard) as a "Continental" stick with which to beat the "positivists."

Philosophy has become a battleground of proscientific versus antipositivist positions primarily in the anglophone world. The philosophy of the 1970s and 1980s in England and America has been called "postpositivist," but it is not clear that it is "postanalytical." The ordinary language wing was in conflict with the logical positivists from early on. In recent decades, analytical philosophy has been getting both more metaphysical and more technical, with the development of possible world logics, explorations of foundations of mathematics, and both realist and antirealist ontologies. The analytical/positivist coalition of mid-century which used to ridicule Continental existentialism and Marxism has dissolved, and previously taboo influences have been flowing in.

Contemporary anglophone philosophy seems to be in flux, with no clearly dominant position. In considerable part this seems due to the internal dissolution of the old logical positivism. Few anglophone philosophers endorse Parisian antipositivist movements with the fervor found in literature departments. Lamont (1987) shows this pattern in the career of Jacques Derrida. Derrida's first success came by appealing to nonacademic literary journals in the 1960s. He used much the same the cultural capital (Nietzsche, Heidegger, Husserl) as the previous generation of existentialist philosophers, who had by then been upstaged in France by the structuralists; Derrida redirected this material towards elevating the textual concerns of the critics and undercutting the conception of philosophy as an autonomous discipline. This is a central theme of deconstruction, attacking the "logocentrism" of the philosophical tradition. Derrida's reputation declined in France after the radical student movement faded in the 1970s (as one can see from the citation patterns given in Lamont 1987), but it took off in American academic publications in the mid-1970s and especially the 1980s. Antipositivist philosophy is to a considerable extent a border crossing, both across disciplines and across national academic systems. Here the key pattern is not from French into anglophone philosophy, but from the alliance of literature and philosophy which originated in the crisis of the French academic world in the 1960s (Bourdieu 1988), flowing into American literature departments undergoing a crisis of their own.

Fine Arts.

One might expect that the fine arts would be centers of antipositivism, especially since a general hostility to science has been part of the ideology of most artistic movements during the twentieth century. Moreover, the term "postmodernism" originated as a technical usage for distinguishing periods of architectural style, before it was blown up into a slogan for a wider movement. Nevertheless, academic specialists in the fine arts appear to be divided between proponents and opponents of the postmodernist philosophies. One wing consists of museum curators and other experts in art history; their work continues to have a strongly empiricist direction, since it depends on examining evidence for dating and authenticating works of art, establishing their provenance, and sometimes engaging in technical work of art restoration.

The world of museums has generally been expanding and prospering, and thus the material basis for careers in this "empiricist" side of the fine arts has been strong, with little motivation to admit new ideologies, especially those which undermine the traditional work of art curators. On the other side, art critics share some of the same problems as literary critics: the classics in their subject matter have been studied for generations, while the focus of contemporary art is extremely dispersed. Thus the struggle for attention among the critical interpreters of art is served by focusing on a metatheory of interpretation in itself, imported from the larger transdisciplinary movement of postmodernism.

The fact that the fine arts have become a battleground, rather than automatically a stronghold of antipositivism, indicates that the crucial factor is not simply one of cultural contents. It is not simply that "soft" fields are inherently antipositivist, whereas "hard" fields pursue scientific methods. This is illustrated by the history of artists' ideologies. In the Renaissance, painters and sculptors were generally in the forefront of the scientific and mathematical movement, as the careers of Piero della Francesca, Leonardo da Vinci, and Brunelleschi remind us. Although the romanticist movement in art turned antiscientific in its ideology, there were proscience themes associated with movements such as the impressionists, pointellists, and futurists. The alliance of aesthetics with antipositivism is a particular coalition that needs to be explained by social conditions in particular sectors of the intellectual world. The split within fine arts departments in the late twentieth century suggests that conditions affecting the careers of art curators and interpreters are largely responsible for whether they import ideological movements such as deconstructionism.

Political Science.

Political science is a battleground swept by movements from different sides of the academic world. The imperialism of rational choice models from economics has become extremely influential. There were versions of this already in the 1950s and 1960s with game theory and economic models (Rapoport, Riker, Downs); the movement has become increasingly strong, and has invaded the domains of policy and political philosophy (Buchanan, Rawls). Evolutionist, sociobiological, and psychological models also flow in from the positivist side. Political science also has been fertile ground for many variants of contemporary antipositivism. Particularistic and relativistic history of ideas (e.g., Quentin Skinner) have welcomed the support of deconstructionist philosophy; the semiotic or "linguistic turn" has found sympathizers in political theory.

Political science was always thematically divided among its various branches: constitutional and judicial philosophy, research on political behavior and administrative organization, history of political ideas, political development. In one direction it overlaps with empirical sociology, in another with philosophy and law. These traditional divisions seem to be the lines along which the current battleground is shaped between positivist and antipositivist positions; while the content of these positions today is not so much generated within but imported from broader movements outside.

Sociology.

Sociology too has its long-standing internal splits: applied and basic research; quantitative and qualitative methods; ideological activism and value-neutrality; history of ideas; theory with and without research; research with and without theory; not to mention a host of substantive specializations and differences in theories. There have been both highly positivist and antipositivist positions in sociology since the 1920 and 1930s (the Ogburn/Lundberg camp versus Blumerian symbolic interactionism, to name just one). U.S. sociology has repeatedly imported many of the broader intellectual movements on both sides of this battle. We have already seen that the logical positivists provided the exemplary textbooks for scientific methodologists in the 1950s and 1960s; at the same time, ethnomethodology imported the antipositivist stance of German phenomenology. Since the 1970s, sociology has experienced all the strong interdisciplinary movements: rational choice economics, sociobiology, population genetics on one side; the variants of Continental Marxism and post-Marxism (the Frankfurt school, structuralist Marxism, and the cynical post-Marxist themes that make up postmodernism); the "linguistic-cultural turn" of literary theory, semiotics and deconstructionism.

We lack a clear estimate of the strength of these various movements within sociology. It would appear that the economic and to a lesser degree the biological models have found their niches in particular areas of research and even in sociological theory, although they have plenty of competition from indigenous sociological models. The antipositivist movements seem to be strongest among specialists in theory (especially those who reject any combination of theory with empirical research). Among researchers, antipositivist ideas are strongest in the rapidly expanding sociology of culture (although some sociologists here also pursue systematic explanations) and in some areas of historical sociology.

One other segment of sociology which is quite sympathetic to antipositivist ideas is feminist sociology. Although there are proponents of feminist politics who work in a variety of methodological positions, the label of "feminist theory" has generally been appropriated by those who identify their standpoint with a rejection of science and often of objectivity as well, and denounce these as male perspectives. Sometimes a united front is propounded in which non-European ethnic groups, together with women, are held to have a distinctive form of intuitive, nonlinear thinking, which opposes the moral and cognitive imperialism of Western males. These themes are typically argued in the terminology of current European antipositivism, especially the movements of French intellectuals, who are mostly male. The correlation male/female with positivist/antipositivist does not hold up very well. Not all feminists are antipositivist; feminists in fields such as economics and psychology appear to follow the predominant methods of their fields, and many feminist researchers in sociology follow scientific methods of data analysis and theory modelling. It appears that feminist politics forms a coalition with whatever compatible movements there are within a given discipline. In fields which are highly antipositivist, such as literature or anthropology, feminists assimilate their position to deconstructionism or postmodernism; in positivistic fields they follow the prevailing methods; in battleground fields like sociology, philosophy, and political science, many feminists ally with the antipositivist incursion.

EXPLAINING WHICH FIELDS ARE ANTIPOSITIVIST

There are several candidates for explaining the antipositivist movements which have become so intense in the 1970s and 1980s. One is the left-wing student movement of the 1960s, which lasted into the early 1970s. Such a movement would not have had much intellectual impact until the graduate students who participated in it attained their degrees; thereafter they could continue for several decades publishing works based on the left-wing and anti-academic ideology of the earlier student counterculture. The problem with this explanation is that it does not explain the antipositivism of cohorts after about 1980, when antipositivist ideas apparently picked up steam. Nor does it explain why some fields have been largely immune to antipositivism, while others have embraced it or become battlegrounds.

Antipositivism does not depend primarily on larger streams in the popular culture, at least not since the counterculture movement more than twenty years ago. Occupational prestige surveys now show that scientists rate at the top of the scale, passing medicine. Student choices of fields of study have favored applied fields such as business administration, remote from antitechnicist ideologies. The antipositivist movements appear to be internal to the academic world, and to specific disciplines within it.

We suggest the following explanation in terms of the internal organization of the universities. Fields which undergo a crisis in their material base become intellectual "soft spots"; their practitioners lose confidence in their own intellectual capital and import ideas from other apparently more successful fields. Fields which are stable or growing remain impervious to outside influences. Fields which are rapidly growing tend to become idea-exporters, imperialistically designing to take over the intellectual turfs or "softer" fields.

This crude explanatory model will need refinement. New ideas full of élan (sociologically speaking, loaded with emotional energy) may also come from outside the lineup of local academic disciplines; French ideas may pour into the British and American academic systems, based on conditions in France which are quite different from conditions in the receiving countries. Bourdieu (1984/88) shows how the massive expansion of student enrollments in France in the 1950s and 1960s disrupted the balance between traditionally dominant and subordinate disciplines, and produced career frustrations among the younger intellectuals in the universities and in the Paris mass media. The popularity of literary/philosophical/social-science hybrids like the ideas of Barthes, Foucault, and Derrida emerged from these conditions in France; their transmission into academic disciplines in other countries, however, depended upon conditions in the places of reception (Lamont 1987). In what follows, we attempt to show that imperialist, impervious, or idea-importing disciplines in the United States are respectively those with growing, stable, or declining academic labor markets during this period.

Figures 1.1–6 show several indications of the prosperity of the social science disciplines, and of several humanistic disciplines, in the United States from the 1960s through the 1980s.

The discipline in worst crisis on these charts is history. Through the 1960s it had the largest number of undergraduate majors and close to the highest production of Ph.D.s. Then history underwent a severe crash from these peaks beginning in the early 1970s, reaching the bottom in the early 1980s. Literature underwent a similar crisis in this period. These are the fields in which outside ideas and methods, from French antipositivism or from elsewhere, made their biggest inroads.

The clearest success story on the charts is economics. In the 1960s it was the second smallest of six social sciences (above only anthropology); by the 1980s it was the second biggest both in undergraduate and graduate students, below only psychology. Professional economists have been slightly more numerous than either sociologists or political scientists ever since 1880; all went uphill sharply since the 1940s, and hit a crisis in the 1970s, with economics taking much less of a beating at that time, ending up with a much larger professional association than the others.[4] Psychology suffered somewhat more than economics from the roller-coaster of student contraction in the late 1970s, but overall its growth pattern has been strong. Psychology was a moderate-sized social science in the 1960s, almost dead even with sociology in undergraduates. When most social sciences grew in the university boom of the 1960s and early 1970s, psychology grew the most and became the largest field by 1975. It has dropped off less sharply than virtually any of the others

FIGURE 1.1.
Bachelor Degree Production in the U.S. for Selected Fields, 1963–64 to 1986–87

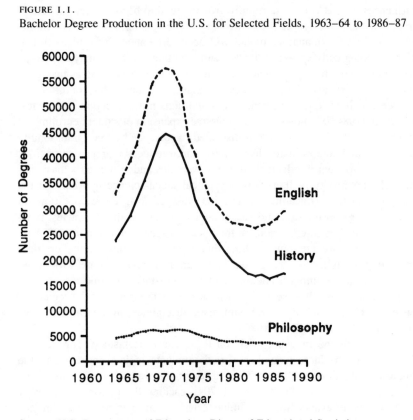

Source: U.S. Department of Education, Digest of Educational Statistics.

since that time, leaving it more than twice as big as its nearest competitor. This atmosphere of success helps explain why economics and psychology were impervious to outside movements, and why economics has been an imperialist idea-exporter.[5]

Moderate crises took place in political science and sociology. Their up-and-down curves for Ph.D.s are very similar from the 1960s through the 1980s; sociology had a rather severe bell-shaped rise-and-fall in undergraduates, largely mirrored by political science. Both had similar sharp rises and sharp drops in professional association memberships. This is in keeping with a characterization as "soft" fields, subjects of rival imperialisms from both the positivist and antipositivist sides.

Anthropology is much smaller field than the other social sciences. It too underwent a crisis in the late 1970s, losing almost half of its undergraduates, but with a milder drop-off in doctorates than other fields. Anthropology had

FIGURE 1.2.
Bachelor Degree Production in the U.S. for Selected Fields, 1963–64 to 1986–87

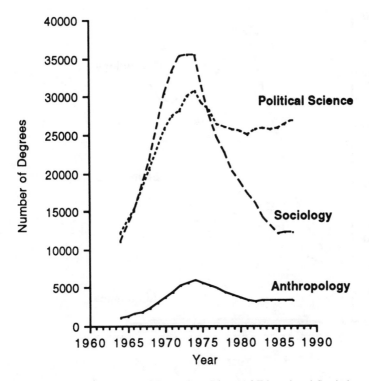

Source: U.S. Department of Education, Digest of Educational Statistics.

another source of strain, experiencing the worse crisis of any social science in its data base, as tribal societies became increasingly unavailable during this period; empirical anthropologists might "migrate back to the mainland" but this put the discipline in danger of losing its identity in sociology. This might help explain why anthropology has been attracted to antipositivist incursions of the literary model, but relatively oblivious to economic imperialism. Anthropology has been only mildly receptive to biological imperialism as well, although this would be an easy step for anthropological subject matter, and biological models existed in anthropology a hundred years earlier. It would appear that the combustion of the two crises: the decline of enrollments, and the loss of its distinctive data base, has turned social anthropology increasingly into an archival discipline like literature; this might explain its affinity to the literary strategy.

FIGURE 1.3.
Bachelor Degree Production in the U.S. for Selected Fields, 1963–64 to 1986–87

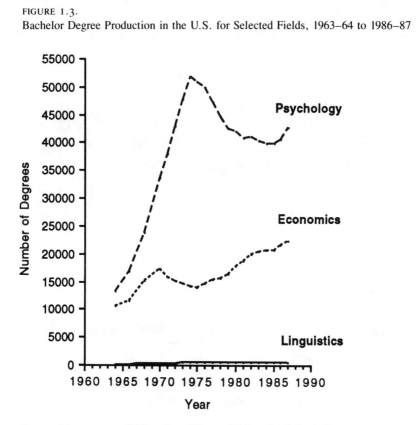

Source: Department of Education, Digest of Educational Statistics.

CONCLUSION

Our general argument has been that fields with strong and expanding academic bases tend to export their paradigms to fields which have weak academic markets. Thus economic and biological imperialism come from expanding disciplines in the United States and overflow into weaker academic departments. The same could be said for the rapidly expanding fields of linguistics, artificial intelligence, and the cognitive revolution originating in psychology. The process may be that scholars in expanding fields are full of self-confidence about their methods and paradigms, while scholars in crisis fields tend to become intellectually self-doubtful; there is so to speak an emotional flow from fields of high intellectual energy into those with low energy.

There is an additional question: why do the imports in some places come from the positivist side, in others from antipositivist movements? Thus in

FIGURE 1.4.
Doctorate Degree Production in the U.S. for Selected Fields, 1963–64 to 1986–87

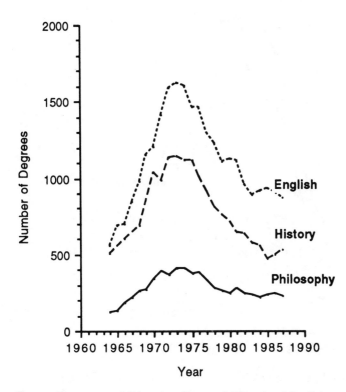

Source: Department of Education, Digest of Educational Statistics.

the American disciplines of literature, anthropology, and history the incursions have been largely antipositivist, coming primarily from movements in France. In U.S. philosophy, on the other hand, positivist programs from linguistics, AI, or rational choice economics have been strong rivals of antipositivist imports, and similar battlegrounds exist in political science and sociology.

Here a second factor enters: the research conditions for pursuing scholarly careers. All of the fields which have become antipositivist strongholds are those which have undergone crises in their research base: literature suffers from exhaustion of its classical texts, and history suffers a similar problem of mining out its traditional subject matter. Analogously, social and cultural anthropology has been threatened with loss of its distinctive research sites, and has turned increasingly into an archive-mining discipline—almost literally

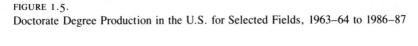

FIGURE 1.5.
Doctorate Degree Production in the U.S. for Selected Fields, 1963–64 to 1986–87

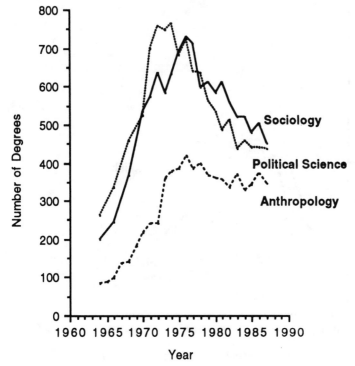

Source: Department of Education, Digest of Educational Statistics.

becoming a textual field. On the other side, political science and sociology also are to some extent textual enterprises poring over their historical archives; but these fields also have abundant arenas for generating new research data. Empirical research enterprises not only keep open a direction for the discoveries necessary for scholarly careers; they also provide immunity from the tendency to regard the world as a text and semiotic interpretation as the privileged method of discourse. Thus one might say that the various metatheories and philosophies, positivist and antipositivist alike, are responses to the conditions of work which scholars face in their particular fields.

One might suppose an alternative explanation: that some fields are intrinsically "hard" or "soft" in their subject matter, or in their long-term traditions, and hence susceptible to incursions respectively from positivist or

FIGURE 1.6.
Doctorate Degree Production in the U.S. for Selected Fields, 1963–64 to 1986–87

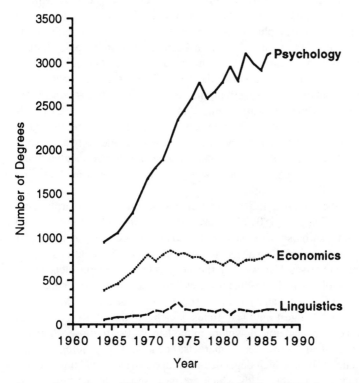

Source: Department of Education, Digest of Educational Statistics.

antipositivist sides. Here the recent experience of the fields of philosophy and of the fine arts provide a crucial comparison. Both of these might be regarded as intrinsically "soft" and textual in their subject matters. Nevertheless academic fine arts departments have been less hospitable to deconstructionist themes than literature departments, and the core of this resistance seems to be grounded in the curators of art works; this is a group with no crisis in their research base, on the contrary bolstered by a boom in museum growth. With philosophy we have no such expanding material base, but the intellectual turf for philosophers has grown precisely with the flow of metapositions across fields. The imperialism of sociobiology or of economic rationality into other academic fields has raise boundary disputes and general issues of the appropriateness of concepts and methods; and these are just the sort of abstract issues with which philosophers are at home. Philosophers have thus been able to claim to contribute to substantive sciences such as biology, economics, or linguistics, but using their distinctive philosophical tools and thus without losing their disciplinary identity. By intervening in the host of issues raised by artificial intelligence, philosophers have even been able to offer some practical relevance; although not itself an empirical research field, philosophy is closer to being an applied field that at any time in its history.

These comparisons suggest that the "hard" or "soft" character of a field's subject matter is not something intrinsically given, but is constituted by the social conditions of work within that field. (cf. Fuchs 1992) Fields become "hard" when a scientific methodology and ideology are applied to them; they become soft when the methods and justifying ideology are textual and interpretative. Fields are battlegrounds between positivism and antipositivism when there are regions within them where both types of methods find bases in the conditions of work.

Why was the scientific trajectory of the social sciences so sharply challenged in the 1970s and 1980s? We have seen that this did not constitute a breakdown into antipositivism across the board; it occurred in particular fields to the degree that their academic markets and their conditions for research underwent crises. Can we push the analysis back one more step, to ask why some disciplines had enrollment crises and others did not? The answer would require a full-scale analysis in the sociology of education. We confine ourselves to one suggestion. The fields which continued to grow even through the general academic downturn in the late 1970s are those which expanded their applied, nonacademic markets: economics, psychology, artificial intelligence. Those which depended most upon strictly academic careers for their graduates are the fields which are most subject to the booms and busts of the academic marketplace; and these are the fields which turned most sharply to antipositivist movements.

Sociology has been a mixed field in this respect. The nonacademic, applied side of sociology has been growing in recent years, although as yet nothing like the huge career markets for economists and psychologists. This applied connection has kept part of sociology tied to a positivist stance, while the more strictly academic part of sociology has felt the problems of university market contractions and the resulting appeals of antipositivist movements. This situation indicates where our current intellectual problems lie. Applied sociology in the past has generally been narrowly practical, not oriented towards the systematic comparisons and cumulative research which are necessary for general explanatory principles; it has been academic sociologists oriented towards the more abstract goals of theory construction who have pushed this program. If the academic side of sociology goes thoroughly antipositivist, the development of general sociological science will tend to become squeezed out between inhospitable poles. An alliance between academic sociologists aiming at general science, and applied sociologists making use of more powerful theoretical tools forged in the academic world, is perhaps the most favorable base from which a scientific sociology might continue to be built.[6]

Notes

1. Etzioni's (1988) recent effort to organize a social economics (largely from the side of sociology) is not so much antipositivist as politically liberal in opposition to conservative market policies; substantively it moves towards propositionalizing traditional institutional economics. A more radical move to displace the economic market model with a social network model by White (1981) is stated in an extremely technical style.

2. A key item which makes a science "hard" is its use of hardware, and its ability to generate formalisms somewhere within its research process, not necessarily at the point of data collection. The sociology of science developed by Whitley (1984) and Fuchs and Turner (1988) indicates why these conditions should affect the organizational structure of a scientific field.

3. The term "poststructuralism" seems to be a peculiarly American one. In France, where the content of these theories originated, the term is not used. It seems to be a conflation of "structuralism" with "postmodernism," indicating the equivalence of these themes within American academic politics.

4. Based on data from American Sociological Association and the American Economic Association.

5. It fails to explain why psychology has *not* been an intellectual imperialist. Further analysis separating the career conditions of academic and clinical psychologists may help elucidate this point.

6. We are indebted for suggestions on previous drafts of this paper to Sam Kaplan, Michele Lamont, and Norbert Wiley.

2

The Failure of Sociology to Institutionalize Cumulative Theorizing

Jonathan Turner

THE SAD TRUTH

In the late 1960s and early 1970s, a spate of "theory construction" books was produced (e.g., Dubin 1969; Blalock 1969; Reynolds 1971; Gibbs 1972; Hage 1972). In retrospect, these efforts amounted to a last-ditch effort to unify the rapidly increasing diversity of sociology under the rubric of theoretical methods that could prove as hegemonic as statistical methods had in the 1950s and 1960s. This intellectual mini-movement failed, and sociology has continued to diversify into ever more subfields and intellectual camps. Theoretical sociology itself illustrates this growing diversity, as new approaches and perspective multiply. Indeed, positivist or scientific theory is now a somewhat beleaguered camp within theoretical sociology, which is an increasingly relativistic and solipsistic subdiscipline. And we might even consider this volume to represent a eulogy to the scientific pretensions of sociology, for in essence these chapters ask: why did formal theory die in sociology?

Formal theorizing did not die, of course, but efforts to develop scientific theories have been seriously wounded. And so, let me rephrase the question: why is there such skepticism about the prospects for scientific sociology in general, and formal theory in particular? My answer to this question is multifaceted. Part of the reason for the failure of formal theory to capture the sociological imagination resides in how sociologists viewed formal theory itself. Another part of the answer is to be found in the history of sociology, especially those historical events that influenced sociology's place within academia and the larger society. And the final part of my answer, which is related to the other two, is to be revealed in the organizational structure of

American sociology as it evolved over the last eighty years. My tale is a sad one; and it troubles me to be the bearer of such depressing news, because I think that it leads to a most unpleasant conclusion: sociology will never be theoretically unified, either by method or substance, and as a result, it will never be considered very important within or outside academia. This is a great tragedy in light of the fact that most of the world's problems are organizational in nature and, hence, are unlikely to benefit from sociological wisdom, especially theoretically informed and codified wisdom about the operative dynamics of the social universe. Let me begin this depressing tale with a look at the advocates of theory construction in the 1960s and early 1970s.

THE EFFORT TO OVERFORMALIZE AMERICAN SOCIOLOGY

From its beginnings, scientific sociology has had a severe case of "physics envy." For although early sociologists propagated analogies to biological organisms, they had a vision for sociology that looked like Newtonian physics. Such pretensions were not only unrealistic, but counterproductive. If physics is the ideal by which a discipline compares itself, it will always be found wanting and inadequate; and, eventually, an overaction against efforts to emulate *any* science would emerge.

Thus, sociology has periodically sought to be formal, but with an image of itself as a kind of social physics. Comte (1830–42) and Spencer (1874–96) certainly had this vision; to a lesser extent, so did Durkheim (1893, 1895); early American sociology texts certainly advocated a science of society that looked very much like physics (e.g., Ward 1883; Gidding 1896; Park and Burgess 1924); and even the sudden concern with formal theory construction in the 1960s and early 1970s revolved around a rather idealized vision of axiomatic theory as the ultimate goal.

The basic problem is that, in a strict sense of this term, sociological theory can never be axiomatic. At best, in Lee Freese's (1980a and b) terms, sociology can develop formal theories, or what I like to call "fake axiomatic" theories. Hans Zetterberg's (1965) important text set the tone, presenting a view of axiomatic theory that does not conform to the dictates of true axiomatic theory (exact classes, definitive concepts, deduction in terms of a formal calculus, capacity to control extraneous interaction effects, etc.).

Even watered-down axiomatic theory, or formal theory, is often beyond our capacity, and it is beyond the capacity of virtually all sciences. Indeed, theory in most sciences is rather loosely stated—often a combination of words and some formalisms. Moreover, "deductions" are what I term "folk deductions" in the sense that a theoretical principle or "law" is intuitively seen to be appropriate for interpreting some set of empirical data. Why, then, should sociology be any different than, say, biology? A good model, I believe, for sociology is the synthetic theory of evolution where key ideas are stated verbally, where only some ideas are formalized with mathematics into models, and where deductions are not elegant or formal but intuitive.

Thus, theory construction books in sociology presented a vision of theory that is rarely realized in science, especially the sciences like biology after which sociology should model itself. Additionally, these theory construction books all communicated a kind of cookbook and mechanical view of theory which was, to say the least, not how theories are created. Theorizing is a creative act, not some lock-step mechanical process. One does not "construct," or "build," a theory like a building. Rather, theories are formalized, when possible, *after* they have been created by intuition and insight. True, some highly formalized theories that come close to meting the criteria of axiomatic theory can generate new insights in using a calculus to make deductions and inferences, but this is rarely the case and certainly not the typical situation in sciences like sociology.

The "theory construction" movement was, therefore, doomed to failure. It communicated an unrealistic and inappropriate ideal; and it sought to reduce theorizing to stilted recipes and protocols. The theory construction movement tried to overformalize sociological thinking; and it is not surprising that sociologists rebelled against it. Moreover, since theory construction abilities could not open clear employment prospects or offer secure financial backing in the same way as statistics (i.e., jobs in data analysis), it could not be successfully rammed down the throats of students in the same way as statistics. Hence, unlike statistics, theory construction was gradually dropped from the curriculum of graduate programs. Of course, the baby was often thrown out with the bathwater because there is an increasing sense in sociology that formal theory—and certainly theory that seeks to be scientific—is not possible or useful. The theory construction movement was thus partly responsible for its own demise, and for the growing antitheoretical stance of much American sociology, but the movement arose and failed in an academic and institutional context. Events in this context, as they had evolved since American sociology's beginnings in the latter part of the nineteenth century, are perhaps far more significant for sociology's failure to accept a vision of itself as a theoretically informed science. The compulsive quality of "theory building" advocacy certainly did not help matters, but the root of the problem goes back to the beginnings of American sociology and to the way sociology became organized in its institutional environment.

THE EMERGENCE AND DISINTEGRATION OF AMERICAN SOCIOLOGY

Implications for Formal Theorizing

Any kind of activity, including intellectual pursuits, requires a resource base—material, symbolic, and organizational (Turner and Turner 1990). By symbolic resources, I refer to the capacity of a discipline to display stores of accumulated knowledge, to maintain common definitions of important problems, to agree upon relevant procedures, and to develop (in the case of sciences) theoretical principles about crucial processes. And, it must evidence practitioners who: (*a*) see themselves as members of the same community; (*b*) share common intellectual goals; (*c*) utilize certain discursive forms; and (*d*) agree upon standards and criteria of adequacy. By material resources, I refer to the ability of a field to mobilize and control the monies, clients, facilities, equipment, and labor needed to conduct intellectual activity. For academic fields, the most relevant material resources are research funds, university facilities, and student bodies. By organizational resources, I mean the success with which a discipline (*a*) can develop coherent patterns of structural interconnection and mutual dependence among its members; (*b*) create mechanisms of decision-making, administration, and control over its members; and (*c*) implement effective means for reproduction of members.

The history of American sociology revolves around efforts to secure symbolic, material, and organizational resources. The early efforts in Europe to see sociology as "social physics" and to analogize to biology can be seen as an attempt to borrow and utilize legitimating symbolic resources from more prestigious sciences. Indeed, the founding fathers of American sociology—Lester Ward, William Graham Sumner, Franklin Giddings, and Albion Small—were never trained in sociology and, except for Ward, they were not even trained as scientists. The result was that they all sought to use science as a legitimating resource, but they did not know very much about it or, at the very least, they had vastly different conceptions about the nature of theory and scientific sociology. They repressed their differences in order to forge a discipline, and they gave extensive lip service in their early texts to Comte, Spencer, and scientific sociology. Their books are filled wtih "principles" and "laws" of what were perceived to be the fundamental properties of the social universe.

But this scientism and emphasis on theory glossed over some major problems in early American sociology's resource base. Materially, the basic resource of early sociology was students who were interested in amelioration. Organizationally within academia, sociology created a niche for itself by taking over the moral, philosophical, and ameliorative leftovers from traditional disciplines. Early sociology—say, between 1890 and 1910—was thus dependent upon religious-based reform movements for its students and a diverse mixture of philosophical reform, practical and applied courses which other disciplines no longer wanted to teach, or which could generate enough student demand to justify the existence of sociologists within American academia.

This material and organizational resource base always stood in tension with the scientism and theoretical preachings of early sociologists, creating a very strange mix of positivism, evolutionism, organicism and implicit functionalism, and interventionism/reformism. Furthermore, reformism and courses intended to appeal to students' reformist sympathies represented a very unstable resource base, for such resources come and go with ever-shifting political and social climates. Yet, to this very day, students' concerns for "practice," "social problems," and "reform" are what attract them to sociology, a situation which sustains the tensions within American sociology and which, inevitably, places limits on how abstract and formal sociology can become.

Partly in response to sociology's vulnerability, the American Sociological Society (ASS) was formed in 1905. This formation can be seen as an effort to secure a more stable organizational resource base. Yet, the founders and the initial membership of 200 individuals were not symbolically unified. Moreover, many of the key members from the two dominant academic departments—Chicago and Columbia—continued their association and activity in other associations, such as the American Statistical Association, the American Economics Association, and the American Political Science Association. ASS was not, therefore, a very strong resource base, and it was filled with members with repressed intellectual differences. These were smothered over with a heavy emphasis on science and abstract theory, but by the end of World War I, the diversity of intellectual commitments could not be glossed over so easily.

Part of the reason for this inability to sustain the Comtean and Spencerian vision was intellectual: evolutionism as a legitimate mode of thinking was on the decline (Turner and Maryanski 1979). But far more important was a dramatic shift in sociology's material resource base. New sources of funding for sociological activity were secured from private foundations, the most important of which was the one supported by the Rockefeller family (Turner and Turner 1990). John D. Rockefeller wanted "realistic" studies, and this request was backed up by funds channelled through institutes and councils (for example, the Social Science Research Council was created and funded by Rockefeller money). This new material base encouraged dissertations, books, and articles that were statistical and quantitative, for Rockefeller wanted "realistic" research rather than speculative theory and moralizing. As a consequence, the quantitative/statistical movement, which had been initiated by Franklin Giddings at Columbia and his early students, began to spread; and with the arrival of Columbia's William Ogburn at Chicago in the late 1920s, Giddings' brand of statistical analysis could now be said to dominate the major centers of sociology on the East Coast and in the Midwest.

The major problem with this line of emphasis is that sociology's other material base—reform-oriented students—often found the increasing quantitative bias of sociology to be frustrating. And, when Rockefeller suddenly withdrew his monies from social science in general, and sociology in particular, the tension between students and researchers was aggravated.

This tension was intensified by the failure of the lead departments of Chicago and Columbia to create replicable and sustainable models of sociological inquiry. The success of their programs was, in large part, the result of the personal charisma of individuals like Giddings, Park, Ogburn and others to mold reformist-oriented students into hard-nosed researchers, but these same figures failed to create academic structures that would fully institutionalize the transformation of reformist students into quantitative researchers. Equally significant, all of this new quantitative activity did not produce very much that could symbolically unify the discipline. There were no cumulative facts emerging in the 1920s and 1930s; there was no accepted body of theoretical principles and, in reality, there was very little theory at all, except for human ecology and symbolic interactionism; and there was no resolution of the tension between science and policy (or reform). Organizationally, sociology did make inroads into academia, but the lead departments only controlled prestige; they did not develop organizational networks, nor did they have control of material resources, with the result that they did not exert a significant unifying force, save for the emphasis on statistical methods. The ASS similarly could not exert great control, as membership dropped dramatically during the 1930s and as the regional associations made their appearance as a rival set of organizational bases.

The result was that, by the 1940s, American sociology had failed to secure a stable resource base, either organizationally, materially, or symbolically. It had no accepted theory, or even epistemology and ontology; it had no accumulated body of knowledge to parade before clients; it had no clear and powerful organizational networks; it had no firm material base, save for student interest in reform and various clients' interest in quantitatively arrayed data. Thus, on the eve of its sudden growth, especially its material base of student enrollments and research funding, American sociology was not a coherent discipline.

When dramatic growth occurred in the 1960s, it encouraged differentiation, diversity, and fragmentation. Except for a brief period of functional theoretical prominence and a continued (and often force-fed) emphasis on quantitative methods, there was nothing to hold the discipline together, and so, it diversified even further (Turner 1989a). And when the sudden collapse of student enrollments and government funding of research occurred in the early 1970s, consolidation did not follow. Instead, the American Sociological Association (ASA) adopted a co-optive strategy, creating new sections, programs, and journals for any group willing to pay dues. More broadly, academics found that they could survive and prosper in narrow intellectual niches by tailoring department curriculums to their interests and creating new specialty journals, professional associations, and informal networks among like-minded colleagues—a situation that only escalated the ASA's cooptive efforts to keep its members from bolting to new specialty associations. And symbolically, theory proliferated into so many diverse schools and perspectives that it added little intellectual unity to the profession. Only quantitative sociology, which continued to exist in tension with the vast majority of students' interests and needs, provided some unifying symbols.

It is in this context that the formal theory movement must be viewed. It came at the very peak of sociology's affluence—money and students—and right before the big crash. It represented an effort to do for theory what quantamania had done for research: to create standardized protocols for abstract thinking and expression; and like statistics, these were to be shoved down the throats of the reformist-oriented students of the 1960s and early 1970s. The movement was doomed to failure because it had no resource base. It was symbolically naive and idealized, presenting a view of theory rarely matched even in the hard sciences; it was unable to secure a material base of clients, whether interested students or monied organizations willing to buy formal theorizing; and it made an implicit alliance with a type of quantitative methods (sampling, scaling, and aggregating individual responses into variables) which was to prove incapable of testing most interesting theoretical ideas. It inevitably failed as a movement; and sociology is better off for this. But, in failing, the idea of developing scientific theory was also questioned, perhaps because of guilt by association with compulsive cookbook approaches to developing theory.

There is a great tragedy here, because the term "sociology" has become a label for a very diverse group of academics who have little in common intellectually and who are increasingly suspicious of all formal theory. Yet, the collapse of the theory construction movement was as much a symptom as cause of formal scientific theorizing's problems. The problems, or potential for problems, were there from sociology's very beginnings, as the founding fathers of the ASS used Comte's and Spencer's positivism to gloss over their differences and to mobilize symbolic resources in an unstable resource situation. It is doubtful that sociology ever could have developed a coherent body of accepted theoretical principles, given its shaky start and its uneven development. As a consequence, the organizational conditions promoting theoretical unity never existed for American sociology. Hence, efforts at unifying the discipline with formal scientific theory would, and will, always fail. Let me pursue this latter theme in more detail.

FORMAL THEORIZING AND ORGANIZATIONAL CONTROL STRUCTURES

Many have commented on the immaturity of sociological theory, but surprisingly, comparatively few have seen the lack of consensus over formal theoretical principles as linked to the organization of sociology. There is now a huge literature on the sociology of science, but relatively little on the sociology of scientific sociology. Instead, the problems of developing formal theory are usually couched in epistemological terms, where in fact, they should be viewed as an inevitable consequence of how sociology, especially in America but elsewhere as well, is organized.

Richard Whitley's (1984) more general discussion can be revised and adopted, I believe, for the analysis of sociology's problems in developing formal theory (Fuchs and Turner 1986). Several conditions are crucial, I believe, to creating an organizational context that encourages and accepts formal theorizing. If actually implemented, most of these variable conditions would be offensive to sociologists who, for all their collectivist biases at the ideological level, are one of the largest collections of "rugged individuals" at the behavioral and organizational level. What I am asserting is this: Mature and formal theorizing are the result of levels of organizational control that most sociologists would never be willing to accept or tolerate. Adopting Whitley's argument for our purposes (Fuchs and Turner 1986), the capacity to generate formal theory and to codify as well as cumulate knowledge have little to do with epistemology, ontology, or methodology but a great deal to do with whether or not a professional organization can:

1. Exclude the lay public from influencing knowledge production.
2. Exclude competing organizations from having legitimate claims on knowledge production.
3. Concentrate control and administration of those resources necessary for knowledge production.
4. Control what is defined as legitimate and important research as well as the credits, prestige, honor, and reputations that go with performing research.
5. Create dense and centralized networks of mutual dependence of resources for performing intellectual work.
6. Reduce task uncertainty by creating consensus over what realms and problems are relevant and important for knowledge production.

7. Create hierarchical bureaucratic structures that control the distribution of resources necessary for knowledge production, as well as the networks of mutual dependence among knowledge producers.

8. Standardize cognitive orientations and criteria for defining intellectual problems.

Under these conditions, and the mutual effects among these variables as outlined in figure 2.1, a discipline is more likely to produce bodies of formal theoretical principles that organize knowledge production with respect to definitions of problems, modes of research, and bodies of cumulated knowledge. Those disciplines, on the other hand, that cannot exclude the lay public and competing organizations, that fail to concentrate resources, that have difficulty controlling the allocation of prestige, that cannot create dense networks of mutual dependence, that are incapable of reducing task uncertainty, that resist hierarchy and bureaucratic control, and that view cognitive standardizing as threatening, will not be able to develop formal theories that guide research and circumscribe knowledge cumulation.

For all these variable conditions, sociology scores in the wrong direction. Sociology has never been able to exclude the lay public from viewing itself capable of producing comparable knowledge; sociology has never been able to exclude competing organizations, and in fact, in the area where it once enjoyed supremacy (quantitative survey research) it has been losing out to private polling and research firms; sociology has never been able to control resource distribution, for resources have come from outside sources (private foundations and government agencies) which have paid little heed to ASS or ASA; sociology has never controlled the allocation of prestige, especially as increasing numbers of journals and professional associations have provided alternative (to ASA) sources of credit, honor, and prestige; sociology has never developed dense networks of mutual dependence for resources, even during the reign of Chicago and Columbia, and today the proliferation of specialty associations, ASA sections, and journals assures that these networks will not develop across the discipline; sociology has resisted narrowing its definition of important problems, and in practice, it has increasingly defined just about any social phenomenon as relevant and important; sociology has failed to exert bureaucratic control over credentials, funding, job markets, membership, journals, and prestige, preferring instead to adopt a cooptive strategy of offering a home for just about everyone who will pay dues and virtually any kind of intellectual activity; and as a result, sociology has failed miserably in cognitive standardization, opting for diversity, pluralism, and multiple paradigms.

How could formal theory survive in such an environment? It can survive, but as only one of many competing kinds of intellectual activity. It could

FIGURE 2.1:
The Organizational Dynamics of Intellectual Activity

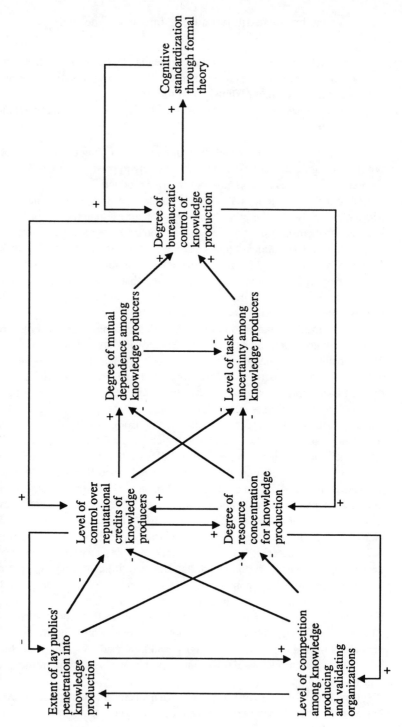

never define problems and organize findings in a field with sixty or so specialty areas that exist more for practical and applied than for theoretical reasons and that operate under different ontological, methodological, and epistemological assumptions. And so, theory of any kind could never organize knowledge production and cumulation in a field where research occurs for purposes unrelated to science and where funding comes from many diverse sources.

What this analysis emphasizes is that there is no problem producing formal theory, per se. In fact, a great deal of exciting and potentially useful theory is produced, despite the tendency of most theorists to seek comfort in metatheory, history of ideas, philosophy, and ideological advocacy. The real problem is that theoretical principles can never guide a profession that is big, diverse, and loosely organized. I once remarked that sociology would never recognize its Einstein, if it had one, because there would be quarrels over epistemology, ontology, and methodology, and over the general "relevance" and "usefulness" of theoretical principles that explained significant portions of the social universe. This is also true for more modest formal theories, for much the same reason.

CONCLUSION

Sociology as it became institutionalized in this country has created a set of structural and cultural obstacles to formal theory. The theory construction movement did not help matters by its overly idealized and rigid view of theorizing, but it illustrates the problems to be encountered in efforts at cognitive standardization in a field which is not insulated from external publics and organizations and which is typified by enormous diversity, loose networks, alternative sources of prestige, reform-oriented students as its most stable resource base, and rugged individualists as its practitioners (many of whom preach collectivism for everybody but themselves).

It is for these reasons, then, that I proclaim sociology to be "the impossible science," not for epistemological or ontological reasons but for organizational and cultural reasons. This is, of course, a great tragedy because it has allowed the one social science that is organized to produce formal theory—economics—to dominate policy and decision-making. It would be far better if sociology had this dominant role, but it is a testimony to the power of theoretical unity that a well organized discipline with the wrong theory can have so much influence on our daily lives.

3

Sociological Theory: Complex, Fragmented, and Politicized

Jerald Hage

In attempting to understand both why sociology has little formal theory and why the theory construction books of the late 1960s and early 1970s did not find a receptive audience, it is useful to contrast sociology with other social science disciplines. Economics and psychology have continued to build intellectually across the decades, as Collins and Wallet suggest in their contribution to this volume. This then poses the question of why sociology is not capable of developing rigorous theory of similar scope, predictive power and practical utility (see Gibbs in part 2), in many if not most areas.

Consistent with one intellectual tradition, in formal theory, I propose to begin my explanation about why the formal theory construction largely failed by making two assumptions. *The first premise is that economic man and woman is easier to theorize about and to research on than sociological man and woman.* As is well known, the laws of demand and supply deal with rational calculations and the pursuit of profit. I believe that rational forms of human interaction are much easier to explain than nonrational, altruistic, or committed interaction. This is not to say that social laws about these topics are impossible, but only that they require more complex theories. Elements involved in the decision to purchase a pin—Adam Smith's famous example—are much simpler than those involved in the choice of a spouse. Economic markets as an institution are much easier to theorize about than organizational structures and the politics within them.[1] Money is easy to count and data relevant to it—trade, tax collection, production figures, and population enumerations—has been available for several centuries. Power, class, and the division of labor, on the other hand, are more difficult to operationalize than pay, income distributions, and gross national product. Therefore, sociological theories involving such concepts as culture, norms, and status pose enormous problems of measurement, providing one reason why some prefer to avoid empirical research. Consistent with this observation, we find that more formal theories have been generated in those specialties within sociology where concepts are simpler. Examples are exchange theory (Homans 1961) and rational choice theory (Coleman 1990), which themselves are quasi-economic models of men and women.

My second assumption is that much of the failure to develop formal sociological theory has emanated from the lack of collective effort to write sociology. There have been few sustained efforts by groups of individuals to build theory in a particular arena. The work in social psychology such as expectations state theory and exchange theory (see the contribution by Cohen) stands out as the major exception but one that proves the premise.

The thrust of this essay is an attempt to explain why there has been so little collective effort. One obvious reason is that in the past several decades sociology has been fragmented and politicized. But the ideological upheavals of the 1960s and 1970s were not the only reasons for the demise of formal theory even though they helped make sociology a battleground for positivism and antipositivism. The inherent complexity of our social reality as reflected in its multiple origins of our founding fathers—Marx, Weber, Durkheim, and Simmel—meant that the discipline started without an integrative paradigm or cognitive framework (see Turner). Furthermore, the lack of state funding of sociological research and other historical factors exacerbated this general condition in the past two decades.

These two assumptions are interrelated. The more one accepts the complexity of social life, the more collective effort becomes necessary in order to construct theories. As is well known in the small groups literature, the more complex the problem, the more effective group solutions are for finding solutions. Constructing theory is not an exception. For a discipline whose raison d'être is groups, there is a certain irony in the absence of collective efforts to construct theory. We need groups of theorists working on the same issues. A good example would be the group led by Wallerstein, which is working on world systems theory at Binghampon, N.Y.

Nor is social reality static. Therefore across time, our perceptions of it are becoming more and more complex. Changing perceptions are coercing scientists to construct theories and perform research in teams. *Science* recently published the count of joint authorships in thousands of journals across all of the sciences including the social sciences. Not unexpectedly, single authorships have declined. Most striking is the climb in the number of articles authored by three or more people, underscoring the movement towards group research and writing. This same tendency is observable in sociology journals today, but was not a characteristic of the 1960s when the theory construction movement started.

TABLE 3.1

Kinds of Sociological Theories and Some Major Ideas for the Demise of Formal
Theory Construction in Sociology

	Objective	*Subjective*
Micro:	Extreme specialization prevent- ing theory development	Ideological and political con- flict
Macro:	Lack of an integrative paradigm Long economic cycles Nature of sociological phenom- enon	Historical origins American state
	Generalizing	*Particularizing*

Source: Adapted from Ritzer (1983). Also see Van de Ven (1981).

The reasons for the lack of collective effort are detailed below. Each of
them represents a different paradigmatic answer. To provide some coherence
to this discussion, I will follow George Ritzer's scheme for characterizing different theories on sociology (see table 3.1) as either micro-objective and subjective, or macro-objective and subjective. Clearly not all the theoretical
paradigms have been represented, but structural and political theories in organizations at the micro level, and institutional, historical, and cultural theories at the macro or societal level represent a good sampling of current work
in the major journals. Within these perspectives are concepts and sometimes
even theories that can help explain why sociology has failed in many areas
(see the contribution by Cohen in the next chapter, which takes a different
slant) to develop formal theory.

MICRO-OBJECTIVE EXPLANATIONS: EXTREME
SPECIALIZATION AND FRAGMENTATION IN THE
INTELLECTUAL DIVISION OF LABOR

To begin our analysis of the demise of the theory construction "movement,"
I choose a well-substantiated theory from organizations. Simultaneously with
the publication of Stinchcombe's (1968) *Constructing Social Theories*,
Lawrence and Lorsch (1967) argued that as specialization in organizations
increased, social integration had to increase as well if the organization was to
be effective. I would argue that this same law applies to the discipline of sociology. If we are to be effective in building theory, we must integrate across
specialties, even paradigms or theoretical frameworks. One possible place for
this to occur is within our departments of sociology.

All disciplines over time become more specialized. But sociology has
perhaps moved too far, too fast during the 1960s and 1970s, creating what
Durkheim (1893) would have called an anomic division of labor.[2] We now

have a large number of people working in many different areas, yet few who carry a common language and can share some basic principles and perspectives. As recently as 1989, the *New York Times,* in its article on the annual American Sociological Association (ASA) meetings, commented on the wide diversity of papers around relatively narrow topics and the general lack of themes.

The fragmentation of the field is perhaps most apparent in the separation between the theory section and the methodology section of the ASA, each of which contains individuals with diverse specialized interests. It is not unusual for our methodologists to specialize in a particular technique, whether event history analysis, time series, panel analysis, lisrel, and so on (see Sage series), or for "theorists" to specialize in a particular theorist, whether this be Marx, Weber, Durkheim, Simmel, Parsons, or whomever.

Perhaps the best illustration of narrow specialization is our graduate programs. Most of them consist of a series of courses in which theory, statistics, data collection methods, research design, and the like are taught largely independently of the other parts of the curriculum (see Cohen 1989). For graduate students, these disparate areas of sociological work, rather than being integrated into a program, remain unconnected compartments, furthering the separation of these areas of the discipline across time. How many classical theory courses relate current research to the ideas of Marx, Weber, Durkheim, Parsons, and so forth? How many research design, data analysis, and data collection courses are taught from the perspective of how to better test the hypotheses of Marx, Weber, Durkheim, Simmel, and Parsons? Such fragmentation slows the development of knowledge in our discipline.

This fragmentation, I believe, is also represented in the many theory construction books that appeared during the late 1960s and early 1970s. Each of them—my own included—tended to emphasize one or another view of theory, but none of them allocated enough space to the problems of integrating theory and research. Furthermore, all of these books reflected the particular substantive issues of the authors, not surprisingly, but ultimately perhaps a fatal weakness. As a consequence, not enough attention was paid in theory construction books to the integration of paradigms, to the combination of research data and theory, and to the analysis of negative evidence. If one or more of these theory construction books had been written by two or more people reflecting the diverse specialties and especially both theoretical and empirical/statistical approaches, would the effort to energize formal theory have been more successful?

Integration involves more than just discussing operational and theoretical definitions; it must deal with the problem of how to handle unexpected findings and, perhaps more critically, the issue of developing relatively abstract hypotheses and even axioms from concrete findings. When this is done, we will likely see a better dialogue between the number crunchers and the concept pushers.

The processes of fragmentation are facilitated by the personnel policies of many sociology departments. Many departments pursued the policy of hiring the best people in a field during the 1970s and 1980s. This has implied building departments around thirty or more relatively narrow specialists, with few of them able to communicate with each other or share interests. Many chairs and recruitment committees still act as if good departments were nothing more than the sum of good people, but thirty good people do not constitute a program of research or theory accumulation. This recruitment strategy adheres to a psychological or economic model of organizations rather than a sociological one, and ignores a large literature on the creative potential of groups, as well as the organizational literature on innovation (see Hage 1980 for a review), because it suggests that a good department is only a collection of good people. Furthermore, we only need to look at what is occurring in the hard sciences to be convinced that carefully built teams produce results.

Why does narrow specialization lead to an absence of attention to the problem of the development of formal deductive theory? Because the asking of small questions rather than big ones prevents the emergence of a theoretical vision. Inductive approaches, especially geared to secondary data analysis, are not likely to encourage the formation of general models of explanation. Although it is contrary to common sense, the development of a discipline moves much faster when broad questions are asked, as the writings of Marx, Darwin, and Freud demonstrated in the nineteenth century.

An opposite but equally pernicious pattern is departmental dedication to "group think," whether this be neofunctionalism, world systems, ethnomethodology, symbolic interactionism, or some other framework. With collective agreement, there is likely to be little questioning of the fundamental assumptions thereby reducing creativity. Nor will there be the reaching out to other perspectives that challenged the assumptions of the prevailing paradigm.

In general, then, there has been in the past too much specialization and not enough integration across specialties, paradigms, and between research methods and theory. Some of the barriers to integration are discussed in the next section of this chapter on micro-subjective reasons. Left unanswered are the reasons for the specialization in sociology, which seems much greater than it is in the other social sciences. To posit too much specialization begs the more provocative issues of why. The analysis of this issue involves a consideration of the nature of sociological knowledge, its origins, and the specific characteristics of American society.

MICRO-SUBJECTIVE EXPLANATIONS: EXTREME POLITICIZATION AND IDEOLOGICAL CONFLICT

In contrast to the structural explanation of specialization and fragmentation, there is a political model of organizations (Pfeffer 1981) that focuses on the conflicts engendered. Fragmentation by itself would not be so adverse, had there not been politicization of the various specialties, and ideological conflict about functionalism or symbolic interactionism.

There are a number of reasons for this politicization, which did not occur to the same extent in economics or psychology during the turbulent sixties and seventies, as Collins and Waller demonstrate.

First, the nature of the recruitment process into sociology changed between the 1950s and 1960s. We began to recruit many people interested in changing society, so as to reduce the social injustices, myself included. There was a boom in the number of students, most of whom had a political agenda. I believe that many of us were first attracted to sociology because of the discipline's emphasis on stratification and were therefore concerned about inequality. This selective recruitment also meant individuals who were more likely to be ideological, that is, true believers in a particular paradigm, neo-Marxism being the most prevalent example during this time period. This same selective recruitment process did not occur as readily in economics and political science, where the issue of inequality is less prominent. Participant observation at national conventions illustrates these recruitment differences. Compare the almost universal choice of suits and ties by men at economic and political science conventions with the frumpy style of male sociologists. Nor should it go unnoticed that the proportion of women in sociology, many of whom are concerned about gender inequality, is much higher than it is in the other two disciplines. The same can be said for minorities. But most fundamentally the specific women, blacks, Hispanics who enter sociology self-selected themselves and are attracted by the theme of inequality.

Second, this recruitment process has had an unfortunate effect on both sociology departments and journals, politicizing both of them. It is hard to be neutral about inequality or other social problems that appear to flow from stratification of classes, genders, and races. There are many examples of sociology departments that have been riddled with conflict by the decision of which specialty to recruit. Furthermore, the compromises have usually been worse. The search for androgynous creatures who cover two areas equally poorly is not a recipe for success. Searching for someone who is good in two specialties, especially since few people qualify, is likely to result in selecting the worst possible candidate.

Politicization also impacted on the nature and the quality of the journals. We have seen the proliferation of many new journals reflecting one or another ideological perspective. None have been concerned with the synthesis of the field. Most of these new journals were founded with the perception that one or another existing journal did not given enough attention to some view. A good example is the *Theory Journal,* which was created because it was felt that the *American Sociological Review* did not provide equal time for theory articles, except perhaps for those involving the reinterpretation of the great masters of yesteryear. As a consequence each section in sociology has obtained its favorite journal and generally has not been receptive to ideas from other perspectives.

Third, the political climate or zeitgeist of the times—Vietnam, racial inequality, feminism, lack of student involvement in university decision-making—inevitably touched most directly on the subject matter near and dear to most sociologists' minds and hearts—social injustices. These issues directly involve societal inequality, and thus the substantive interests of many who selected the discipline of sociology. How many sit-ins occurred in sociology departments as opposed to economic or political science departments? The inevitable consequence was that sociology departments were in many cases not only in the first line of battle *against* the society but usually the major casualty both in the eyes of the university administration and of the larger society. Naturally moral choices require some action but they have left a lasting residue into the eighties, making sociology departments more vulnerable for closure.

One of the major consequences of the struggles of many sociologists to reduce inequalities during the decades of the 1960s and 1970s was the loss of general political support, especially among Republicans. This, coupled with the lack of effective theory, made the critiques of the Reagan presidency and of Senator Proxmire all the more telling. Admittedly their attacks were more broadly based against all social sciences but clearly sociology bore the brunt of it. The cutting of support for sociological research in the National Institute of Mental Health, the National Science Foundation, and other government agencies meant a loss of many job opportunities as well as a curtailment in the development of sociological knowledge.

The ideological conflicts had many ramifications. One of the most dramatic was the creation of new sections in the ASA. Exemplary of this tendency was the fight between the world systems people and the modernization theorists, leading to the establishment of two sections rather than one dialectic, to the detriment of the field and, I might add, the progress of the development of formal theory.

It would be wrong to suggest that the books in theory construction did not play a part. I believe that most of them, when examined from the perspective of today, do read as though they were all written by individuals who believed only in an objective truth and exhibited a strong positivistic bent.

Little was written about historical models, qualitative theory, the problem of exceptions, qualifications by space and time, or what we might call historical/cultural scope conditions (Walker and Cohen 1986). The issue of meaning is given scant attention, nor is the problem of phenomenology addressed at all.

This admission, at least on my part, is important not only because it allows us to understand better the vehemence of the attack by those who held other perspectives during the 1970s but it suggests errors that must be avoided in the future, pointing to what I believe should be the direction of integrative efforts.

MACRO-OBJECTIVE EXPLANATIONS: THE LACK OF AN INTEGRATIVE PARADIGM LONG ECONOMIC CYCLES, AND THE NATURE OF SOCIOLOGICAL PHENOMENA

Macro-objective explanations are concerned with general ideas that are not restrictive to the United States. Hereafter, I propose three interrelated ones, each of which are closely connected, to help understand the lack of collective effort to construct sociological theory. These explanations deal with the prior absence of an integrative paradigm in sociology, and especially paradigms that had considerable predictive power, such as the neoclassical model of market behavior; the impact of long-wave economic cycles on the development of theory; and finally the nature of sociological reality in some objectivist sense. Each of these ideas represents an attempt to construct some theory of knowledge.

The lack of some general integrative paradigm in sociology prior to the appearance of the theory construction "movement" explains both the fragmentation into many specialties and their politicization. Paradoxically much of the ideological conflict describe earlier occurred within an intellectual vacuum. Indeed, it is precisely because sociology was a multiparadigm—but with quite a weak theory rather than compelling predictions in the mid-sixties—that radical critiques were made easier (Ritzer 1990). As we know, ideology grows strongest precisely where ideas are weakest. This, in my opinion, explains in part why economics and psychology were relatively untouched (see Collins and Waller's contribution).

Although many in the 1960s, most notably Gouldner (1970), argued that there was a major paradigm in sociology, namely functionalism, I do not believe that this was the case (see Wiley 1990, 394–96, for another view). Few articles and only one textbook (Johnson 1961) were written from this perspective. Perhaps the major exceptions were two specific areas where functionalism approached something like explanation and prediction: stratification (Davis and Moore 1945) and role theory (Merton 1968). In his review, Ritzer (1975) argues that there were really three competing perspectives during the 1960s and 1970s. Leaving aside whether three is the correct number, his review also argues against the idea of a general paradigm.

If there is no integrative paradigm, then how does knowledge grow? The competitive pressures for distinction lead us to differentiate ourselves from others by constantly searching for something new—which becomes another narrow specialty. In contrast, where there is an integrative paradigm, there is replication, a building of knowledge, and more synthesis. Economics is an example of this latter process, while history is a good example of a field in which extreme specialization has occurred. Within sociology such specialization has followed institutional and conceptual lines. The content of the standard introductory course consists of low-level generalizations about the family, politics, education, and so on. It is this proliferation of discrete arenas without an integrative paradigm that has encouraged the specialization and fragmentation which, as suggested, were one of the basic difficulties in the discipline. A vicious cycle has been established which encourages ever narrowing specialization and makes theoretical intellectual integration more and more difficult. Again, there is little assimilation of facts into generalizations and of these into coherent models or theories. The normal inductive process fails to operate as a consequence for the lack of interrelated research findings. Given this cycle, we do not accumulate theory in the way in which science is expected to.

Equally critical is the fact that the deductive processes of theory construction have failed to operate. No new paradigm has been proposed. To account for this failure, we must turn to another analysis. In a fascinating article Norbert Wiley (1985) has argued for the existence of long waves in theory building corresponding to long economic waves. It suggests that a dominant or general thesis is most likely to be generated when the economy is rapidly expanding. He also believes that sociological theory is likely to be similar to economic thinking during periods of economic expansion. But when the long wave is associated with decline, a large number of antitheses appear. One can describe the periods of 1940–65 and 1965–90 in this fashion, provided one believes that functionalism was the dominant paradigm during 1940–65 (which I have suggested it was not). Regardless, Wiley's thesis does represent another macro-objective reason for the failure of the theory construction movement during the 1970s. Its timing was poor, with its arriving on the scene precisely as the economic expansion of the 50s and 60s was replaced by the stagnation of the 70s and 80s. If I am understanding Wiley correctly, deductive theory and even more generally formal theory will find a more receptive audience during economic expansions while any attempt at generalization is discredited during periods of contraction.

The mechanism involved in Wiley's explanation is not easily explicated, however. One possibility is that in times of economic expansion public optimism is greater, making attempts at theoretical generalizations more accept-able. Furthermore, under these circumstances, the ruling paradigm in economics achieves more legitimacy and sociologists are therefore more likely to be seduced by it, using it in various disguises. Implicit in the func-tional theory of stratification is the predecessor of the human capital argu-ment, which, interestingly enough, burst on the scene in the mid-1960s. Conversely, periods of economic stagnation discredit the economic paradigm and lead people to search for other kinds of answers: phenomenology, social history, and other perspectives that emphasize the differences, exceptions, qualifications, and so forth. It is no accident that power and conflict theory become quite popular during those decades of economic stagnation.

The major reason for the absence of a general integrative paradigm is greater complexity of sociological reality, my first assumption. One of the important insights of Parsons' (Parsons and Bales 1954) last major analytical scheme, the AGIL scheme, is that groups, organizations, institutions, and societies have multiple functions that is the functions of adaptiveness, goal achievement, integration and latency or pattern maintenance, hence the ac-ronym of AGIL; they are not just determined by efficiency considerations as the economists would argue. The recent interest in Etzioni's (1988) book *The Moral Dimension,* I believe, suggests a recognition of this greater complexity in the choices we make.

I might also add that it is this multi-utility of functionalism, its historical origins and its diversity across institutional sectors that is, its complexity, that have made the development of formal theory in the 1950s and 1960s within functionalism more difficult than in economic models of demand and supply.[3]

To summarize, the factionalism of sociology is facilitated by the lack of a single integrative paradigm, encouraging the centrifugal forces to move to-wards greater specialization. Furthermore, texts on theory construction came onto the market at the beginning of a long economic down-cycle when at-tempts at generalizations became suspect, discouraging the development of alternative general perspectives. The inherent multiple utilities involved in social interaction require complex formal sociological theory.

MACRO-SUBJECTIVE EXPLANATIONS: THE HISTORICAL ORIGINS OF SOCIOLOGY AND THE ROLE OF THE AMERICAN STATE IN FUNDING

Macro-subjective explanations focus on particularistic reasons at the societal level. Most typically they revolve around the culture of a country, a specific historical moment and more recently analysis of the institutions of society. In our discussion of the specific recruitment patterns into sociology, we men-tioned a particularly important macro-subjective explanation, namely the zeitgeist of the time. Logically, within the framework of micro and macro, I should discuss this historical explanation because of its society-wide origin. It is, however, so well known that I believe this does not need any elaboration.

As Wiley (1985, 394–95) has cogently argued, the functionalism of the 1960s appeared to be ineffectual at explaining the large and major conflicts occurring in American society at the time. Instead, I want to concentrate on several other macro-subjective explanations that are usually not considered, namely the historical origins of sociology, the American culture belief in individualism as inhibitors of collective efforts to formulate theory, and the absence of state funding of sociological theory building.

The historical origins of sociology provide an enormous insight into the major theme of this essay—namely the lack of an integrative paradigm and the resulting specialization, fragmentation, politicization, and ideological conflicts. Precisely because sociology is more complex and the theoretical questions posed are more difficult, sociology was the last social science discipline to emerge—if we ignore some of the new interdisciplinary areas such as urban, black, and women studies or development, public policy, and the like. In the genealogy of knowledge, the most difficult issues generally emerge last and thus, not surprisingly, sociology appeared only during the nineteenth century (I leave aside Khaldun, because he had little influence on Western thought). If economists date their origin with Adam Smith's opus, we sociologists should not be too disappointed in the progress we have made. Furthermore, we cannot point to a single Adam Smith who laid out the basic sociological issues. Some would credit Marx with being the first sociologist, but he is not the only grandfather. Others would include publication of the first works by Durkheim and by Weber in 1893 (*The Division of Labor*) and 1905 (*The Protestant Ethic and the Spirit of Capitalism*), respectively. Others might add Simmel.

In other words, we do not have a single grandfather (and again I will ignore Comte as irrelevant) but instead a patrimony that spans a considerable range of issues, philosophical assumptions, and ideological concerns. Weber took exception to many of Marx's ideas and a similar implied opposition separates Durkheim from Simmel. Likewise, the difference between Weber and Durkheim could not be more striking.

Thus, rather than one clear and focused beginning, sociology can boast of multiple origins, which in turn has fed different perspectives, making the integration of various specialties, truths, and paradigms more difficult. We did not start with a coherent view of ourselves and our problematic. *This is reflected in the greater complexity of sociology and differentiates our discipline from both economics and political science, whose more limited focus on a single institutional sphere and thus kind of human action allowed them, paradoxically, to be broader in the scope of their theory.* Specialization, fragmentation, and the like have further been exacerbated in the United States because of our culture of individualism carried to its logical extreme. At the other end of the time line, if we turn to the present, the low level of funding by the American state or federal government has contributed to the demise of theory. Not only the scarcity of funds but the fact that when funds are scarce they are made available for practical, not theoretical research, has impacted on the work of theorists. There has been money to study rural poverty, mental illness, teenage pregnancies, crime, drugs, program evaluation, school drop-outs, vocational training, undoubtedly important issues, but the conse-quences for the development of theory have been negative.

Furthermore, we are unlikely to obtain complex solutions if the National Science Foundation funds the sociology section a mere 4 to 5 million dollars a year, much of it going for data collection that is not theoretically informed. In addition, this amount in real terms has been reduced to the present 3 mil-lion. (I have already explained why our funding was cut.) So as our socio-logical reality grows more complex and complicated with many specialties, funding has in fact declined. Under these conditions, even with secondary data analysis, sociological theorizing will not advance much. Please do not assume that I am advocating stopping these efforts or reallocating dollars from them; I believe this would be a serious mistake. I am only asking how far the process of formal theory construction can proceed, if there is a divorce between formal theory and the collection of data to test that theory. Clearly, the "big ticket" projects in the physical and biological sciences are tightly connected to deductive theories, whether this be the theory of the Big Bang or of small DNA. The complexity of sociological research suggests a similar need for theoretically informed research.

CONCLUSION

The untimely demise of the theory construction "movement" does not have a simple answer. I have personally suggested a variety of reasons: micro-objective, micro-subjective, macro-objective, and macro-subjective. The other contributions provide valuable additions with which I find myself largely in agreement.

Despite the large number of explanations provided, in this essay two themes are dominant. The more difficult subject matter of social life resulted in sociology emerging later than economics or political science and with more origin points, which in turn has prevented the development of a com-mon framework, has accounted for the use of the institutional approach in introductory sociology textbooks, and has deprived the discipline from a co-herent cognitive framework (see Turner).[4] This kind of birth has perpetu-ated specialization and fragmentation. The pursuit of different specialties has bifurcated theory and methodology and this in turn led to ideological conflicts over theory, method, and criteria of truth. This state of things was exacerbated by the particular historical moment when the theory construction books were written, drawing into sociology individuals that were especially prone to politicization—as is sociology generally. I believe these ideas help us to understand why economics and psychology were spared the attack on positivism that sociology experienced, and also why the latter was especially vulnerable to this attack (see Collins and Waller).

The lack of resources has exacerbated the specialization and fragmentation. Government funding has followed the fad of the moment, pouring large resources into the many practical problems of the day, few into basic research, and almost none into a collective effort at theory building.

At the beginning, I suggested that, despite the failure of formal theory during the past two decades, my intent was to use this as a starting point for the construction of a general theory of knowledge—at least one applicable across the social sciences. As can be discerned in this essay, the major insight is contained in the two starting assumptions. The more complex reality necessitates a collective effort. But cooperation did not occur for a variety of reasons. Without this collective effort the discipline is condemned to increasing fragmentation, and the failure to accumulate generalizations, theoretical models, and the like. Whether or not this is a permanent, existential condition remains to be seen.

Notes

1. It is of course true that in the past several decades economic models of reasoning have been applied to many noneconomic situations. For example, see Becker (1975) and Williamson (1975).

2. The key point is the number of specialties relative to the number of people in the discipline. It is the large number of specialties despite the small size of the discipline that is striking. Also see Merton (1986, quoted in Ritzer 1990, 2).

3. Despite the extreme criticism of functionalism as favoring stability and a conservative approach, it is precisely the concept of multiple utilities and the impossibility of achieving them that sets up the dynamic of change (see Hage 1965).

4. My own perspective is that there are two implicit themes that could be the basis of some general theoretical framework. One is the theme of inequality or stratification and the other is the themes of groups or collectives, which themselves are not unrelated. In other words, introductory textbooks could be organized around these two themes in each of the institutional sections. Even social psychology and demography could be handled somewhat in this way.

4

Sociological Theory: The Half-full Cup

Bernard P. Cohen

I want to sound a positive note in contrast to the mood suggested by the titles of the other papers in this volume, particularly those that contain the word, "failure" or its synonym, "breakdown." It may come as a surprise that I see the cup of sociological theory as half-full rather than half-empty as the pessimist would see it, but I am convinced that there is a sound basis for the optimist's view.

Tom Fararo recently wrote: "Not long ago many sociologists could feel the truth in the striking metaphor that sociology is tired. . . . But we have entered a new epoch: sociology is revived. It is vigorous" (Fararo 1989). While this view is perhaps more upbeat than warranted, it is certainly true that hand wringing and black armbands are, to say the least, premature. Theory development may not be as flourishing an enterprise as some of us would like, but neither is it moribund.

Assessing the state of theory development requires context and criteria. The purpose of this paper is to propose and apply a set of criteria to theory and theory development.

Note that I avoid the term, "formal theory." I do so since the term is problematic on several grounds: its meaning is ambiguous, it concedes a battle that should not be conceded, and it is bad public relations.

"Formal theory" does not have clear, unambiguous meaning, unless it is regarded as synonymous with "formalized theory." The latter term, however, carries a connotation that allows the separation of a theory from its formalization, where formalization involves putting arguments into symbolic or mathematical form. Since I regard theory development as a process, one stage of which may involve formalization, the possibility of independently examining a theory and its formalization is crucial. It is not clear that "formal theory" allows such separation.

The second problem with the term is that it concedes a battle that I do not want to concede. If what I do is formal theory, then what is informal theory? I don't think the tendency in sociology to treat anything that is not data as theory is appropriate; for something to be a theory, it must meet some criteria. While I am willing to debate what those criteria are, I am not willing to say that anything goes—that any hunch, comment, value judgment, speculation, or ideological exhortation is "theory." The use of "formal theory" implicitly allows an alternative category and one that is vague and unspecified. In so doing, it gives legitimacy to some kinds of efforts that in fact undermine the formulation of explicit, general and testable claims about the social world.

Labeling work as "formal theory" and those who do that work as "formal theorists" is poor public relations. It puts off potential colleagues and comforts opponents. On the one hand, the label deflects some who are doing genuine theoretical work but who are not ready for formalization and it makes them unduly defensive. On the other hand, by labeling something as "formal theory," those who oppose explicit, testable theory can relegate bodies of work to a disciplinary boondocks and ignore them. While sociology as a discipline may allow many tents—and I don't object to that—I see no need for those of us with a scientific orientation to concede most of the theory realm to the nonscientists.

THE PROBLEM OF ASSESSMENT

Now let me turn to issues more central than how we label theoretical work. I assert that a mood of despair over the state of development of explicit, testable sociological theory is unwarranted. (I will also add that it is counterproductive.) Now my statement that despair is unwarranted may simply be an opinion to which I am entitled and with which others are free to disagree. On the other hand, it may be a consequence of applying a set of standards to which many, or most, of us subscribe. If so, my statement—put in less literary language—would approximate a measurement relative to a set of multidimensional criteria. However, establishing the criteria and determining whether or not we share them as not a trivial matter.

Although sociologists make assessments of theory all the time, it is truly remarkable how little attention they pay to the development of explicit criteria for these assessments or to serious analysis of criteria that people use, often implicitly, to make judgments about theories or theoretical development. Developing criteria for judging data analysis continues to be a growth industry, but few people worry about the standards for deciding the merit of ideas. We all make such judgments, but for the most part we make them quite unselfconsciously; we treat them as matters of taste, as value judgments and, thus, as not subject to rational debate. And, we often state our appraisals without feeling any need to justify them, assuming that right-thinking colleagues will share our values and agree with our assessments. Furthermore, many of us subscribe to Kuhn's incommensurability thesis, so we regard it as pointless to try to convince anyone else; if they disagree, they must be operating with a different paradigm.

Now some readers will certainly object, arguing that there are criteria. These objectors will further claim that the criteria are clear, obvious, and widely shared among those of us committed to science. Everyone knows that scientific theories ought to be logical, simple, fruitful, and true. Well, Popper (1959) showed us that "true" wasn't a realizable criterion so we modified that to be "tested and not falsified." Lakatos (1970) and others have raised questions about Popper's criterion as a guide to assessing theoretical development. Popper did, after all, propose falsifiability as a criterion to demarcate science from nonscience and that is not the same thing as evaluating the cognitive status of a theory whose scientific credentials are not in question. On the other hand, Popper also argued that reproducible falsifications were sufficient grounds for the rejection of a theory. Elsewhere, I have shown why Popper's criterion doesn't help the practical task of theory development (Cohen 1989), that is, why it doesn't provide an appropriate standard for deciding when to abandon a theory. The point of this discussion is that none of these obvious criteria, with the possible exception of "logical" provide firm guidelines that cannot be questioned.

If there is no "truth," is "beauty" all that we are left with, a beauty that is in the eyes of the beholder, or those who share his paradigm? Needless to say, I am not an adherent of Kuhn's incommensurability thesis, nor the radical subjectivism that it entails. As Laudan, in his penetrating critique of Kuhn, points out (Laudan 1982), there are shared cognitive values to which we can appeal and which provide rational bases for assessment even if these values do not determine assessments uniquely. If, for example, we hold the cognitive value that theories should be modifiable by evidence,[1] this value will not determine the one best theory but it will certainly allow us to eliminate some theories from consideration.

DEVELOPING A SET OF CRITERIA

The discussion to this point should indicate that the task of developing criteria is not a task that will be accomplished simply and quickly. But it is not a problem that will disappear and, if we want to put our assessments on sounder foundations, it is a problem we must address.

Laudan offers a fruitful starting point:

> The first and essential acid test for any theory is whether it provides acceptable answers to interesting questions: whether, in other words, it pro-

vides satisfactory solutions to important problems. . . . In appraising the merits of theories, it is more important to ask whether they constitute adequate solutions to significant problems than it is to ask whether they are "true," "corroborated," "well-confirmed" or otherwise justifiable within the framework of contemporary epistemology. (1977, 14–15)

Laudan's approach has two important virtues: (1) it locates the criterion problem within the science rather than external to it; and (2) it is pragmatic in that it points to a set of practical standards that can be applied even as they are developed and refined. Determining whether a theory solves a problem is, after all, a matter for content specialists rather than epistemologists, and "bench scientists" usually have a pretty good everyday knowledge of both problems and solutions.

The approach is not without difficulties, however, since one can immediately ask several questions: How does one determine the adequacy of a solution? Who decides what are "interesting questions" and what are "important" or "significant" problems? And it is unlikely that one would want to establish an *a priori* list of interesting or significant problems that acceptable theories must solve. There are many instances of problems becoming interesting or significant *because* a theory solves them. The perihelion of Mercury became interesting and significant because of Relativity Theory not *vice versa*. Moreover, the motivation for a theory is typically a particular question and if the theory did not provide an answer to that question, it would be unlikely to be presented to the discipline. It is reasonable, therefore, to ask how much credit we should give to a theory for answering its motivating question. Finally, seeking what is interesting and significant can lead back to just the kind of subjectivity that some of us criticize in Kuhn's analysis. Nevertheless, these difficulties are likely to prove more tractable than establishing truth criteria for a theory.

Laudan (1977) recognizes most of these traps and offers provisional solutions focussing on the "cognitively rational weighting" of scientific problems. For example, he argues, "If a particular problem has been solved by any viable theory in the domain, then that problem acquires considerable significance; to the extent that any competitor theory in the domain will almost certainly be expected either to solve it or to provide good grounds for failing to solve it" (1977, 33). He discusses a number of other factors which contribute to this weighting and, in a later work, contends that importance is not a matter of individual taste but depends on the "probative significance" of the problem solution (Laudan 1982, 99). I do not believe that his suggestions resolve the issues, but, since the purpose of this paper is not a critique of Laudan, let me finesse the question except to urge people to give very serious thought to it.

My purpose is to build on Laudan's basic directive that we evaluate a theory's success in solving problems in order to formulate some provisional criteria for the assessment of theory development in sociology. In doing this, it is possible to put aside the question of how one determines the importance or significance of a problem solution. While the ultimate success of a program to develop standards for evaluating problem solutions could depend on acceptable answers to such questions, it is nevertheless possible to begin to develop and use criteria even in the absence of an acceptable formulation of "importance." Furthermore, one could argue that "importance" or "significance" may only be evaluatable with the hindsight of a historian of science.

Many sociologists will object to my proposal to postpone issues of "importance" or "significance." These people will insist that acceptable theories must deal with phenomena of central concern to them or to the discipline. There are many agendas and it is always possible to construct an agenda which no theoretical development will satisfy, but it is unreasonable to dismiss a theory which has demonstrated problem-solving effectiveness simply because the theory does not solve any problems that concern the evaluator. If we must assess theoretical development in terms of problem agendas on which there is relatively little consensus among sociologists, then naysaying is inevitable and progress impossible. At our current stage of development, we ought to cheer every successful problem-solving attempt whether or not we think the problem is important and whether or not we regard the substance of the solution as congenial.

Empirical, Conceptual, and Practical Problems

Laudan distinguishes between "conceptual" and "empirical" problems; he writes, "anything about the natural world which strikes us as odd, or otherwise in need of explanation, constitutes an empirical problem" (1977, 15). If a theorist wants to know why some organizations lose sight of their goals, the theorist has an empirical problem.

Conceptual problems are of two types: internal, where a theory exhibits internal inconsistencies or when its basic categories of analysis are vague and unclear; and external, where a theory conflicts with some other theory or doctrine "which proponents of (the given theory) believe to be rationally well founded" (1977, 50–51). An example of external conflict would arise if an exchange theorist formulated a theory which explicitly involved the negation of reinforcement principles, a doctrine that is a key presupposition of exchange theories.

To Laudan's empirical and conceptual problems, I want to add "practical problems." While I will not argue that a theory must have practical applications, theories that do direct engineering operations should get credit for this type of accomplishment; it is certainly the case that utility in solving practical problems has historically played a major role in both assessing and promoting theory construction.

Theories, then, are to be judged according to how well they solve empirical, conceptual, and practical problems within their domain and scope, where domain refers to the substantive content the theory addresses and scope refers to the conditions of applicability of the theory. We can specify many aspects of problem solution involving questions such as: How well do theories explain facts within their domain and scope? How well do they deal with conflicts with other theories that share domain and scope? How well do they provide clarification of ideas? How well they resolve, or at least, recognize internal contradictions? (Laudan proposes deducting the problems a theory generates from those it solves, but I think he is incorrect on this point because some anomalies a theory generates may be fruitful and progressive.)

Theoretical Progress

While one may examine a single theory at a given time point, judgments of that theory must be relative to other available theories, either earlier versions of the same theory or competing theories. In this connection, Laudan's notions of progress and progressive change are particularly useful:

> *Progress can occur if and only if the succession of scientific theories in any domain shows an increasing degree of problem-solving effectiveness.* Localizing the notion of progress to specific situations rather than to large stretches of time, we can say that *any time we modify a theory or replace it by another theory, that change is progressive if and only if the later version is a more effective problem solver . . . than its predecessor.* (1977, 68; emphasis in original)

A focus on progress directs our attention to the context and stage of development of the science to which a theory belongs. A theory's problem solutions must be compared to available alternative solutions including those of its predecessors and its current competitors. Laudan stresses that "*the evaluation of theories is a comparative matter.* What is crucial in any cognitive assessment of a theory is how it fares with respect to its competitors" (1977, 71; emphasis in original).

Progressiveness and comparative assessment fit well with research strategies that promote cumulative research programs. If a theory is to be progressive, it must be a more effective problem solver than its predecessors; one important way this can occur is if the theory has the potential to solve new problems in addition to those addressed by its predecessors or competitors. Using this criterion of progressiveness disposes of a troublesome issue that I raised earlier: Since most theories are formulated in order to solve some problem, how much credit should a theory get for solving that problem? The comparative requirement means that a theory only gets credit if it contains a solution that improves on available alternatives. The progressiveness requirement means that it only gets credit if it has the potential for solving other problems than those which motivated its formulation. Of course, if a theory is the first theory in a domain, it deserves some acclaim; but if the theory is ad hoc in the sense that it solves no other problems than those that motivated it, then that acclaim will be small and short-lived. Even where comparison is not possible because a theory is unique in its domain, there is still a standard for assessment in the requirement that a theory be progressive.

Some formalized theories are one-shot affairs that do not meet the progressiveness criterion and this could explain why people are not interested in these efforts. I have in mind a number of mathematical models that appeared in the 1960s and 1970s and disappeared very quickly. In general, it is no trick to solve the specific problem that motivates a given theory, but it is much more of a trick to formulate that theory so that it provides solutions to a range of distinct problems. While every endeavor to develop a new theory begins as an attempt to solve a particular problem, for the product of that endeavor to be progressive, it must have consequences that go beyond the original question.

Theories, then, are problem-solving instruments and need to be evaluated according to their successful solutions and their capacity to expand the set of problems for which they contain solutions.[2]

SPECIFICATION OF CRITERIA

To evaluate a theory, we inquire about the problems a theory purports to solve, assume that every problem is of sufficient importance to merit our attention and analyze the nature and substance of each of the solutions. We address three questions: (1) Does the theory actually solve the problem? (2) How does the solution compare to available alternative solutions? and (3) Is the solution progressive in that it represents an improvement over its predecessors and in that it opens up possibilities for solving new problems?

These questions entail evaluating a theory on a number of specific dimensions. Many of these are already familiar to us; other dimensions remain to be formulated. For each of these general questions, there are specific criteria to be explored with respect to empirical, conceptual, and practical problems.

A Solution?

In evaluating whether or not a theory solves an empirical problem, we employ criteria to evaluate a theory's claim that it explains or predicts a set of hitherto unexplained, or inadequately explained observations. If the theory is formalized, then one can determine if the observation statements are derivable from the theory. The theory, however, does not have to be formalized, but it does have to be sufficiently explicit so that one can make a reasonable quasi-deductive argument that leads from the theory to the observation set. (Even though a theory is not formalized, it should be possible to use logical analysis to critique parts of the theory.) If one cannot make such an argument, then we must examine whether any modifications to theory will allow the desired inference. On one level, the theory solves the problem when we are willing to accept the reasoning which connects it to the observation set.

There are other criteria that can be invoked in evaluating the adequacy of the theory's solution of an empirical problem. These include: generality of the explanation; scope of the theory; precision of theory's predictions; and substantive criteria that are specific to the domain of the theory. There are also substantive considerations that can be used for theories regardless of domain. Consider two types of explanation, one of which explains a particular observation set by including it in a general class of phenomena, whereas the second explains the set by postulating a mechanism or process which arises from some antecedent conditions and results in an outcome that is represented by the observation set. These are not mutually exclusive; in fact, many explanations involve both types, but each type requires a different analysis. For the first type, one can ask whether or not it is reasonable to consider the particular set as a member of the general class. For example, is it reasonable to treat women executives in the telephone company as "tokens"? The answer requires an analysis of the properties of the concept as well as an analysis of the empirical situation. Raising such questions, of course, generates interesting conceptual problems which the theory as it stands can solve or which a modified theory may be able to solve.

For explanations based on mechanisms or processes, one can examine the way the mechanism is supposed to operate, its internal consistency, and how one determines whether or not it is operating. In cases where a theory postulates unobservable processes, it is particularly important to require that the theory specify conditions that permit the inference that the process is not operating as the theory asserts. Status Characteristic Theory (Berger et al. 1966, 1972) postulates an unobservable, four-stage process by which status differences affect interaction among members of a group; by experimental intervention, one of the early studies created the initial conditions for each of these stages and demonstrated that the same outcome resulted. If that experiment had failed, it would have raised a serious difficulty for the theory regardless of how much other empirical support the theory had because it would have called into question the key explanatory argument of the theory. In other words, the theory would not have solved the problem it purported to solve.

This last example suggests that it is not sufficient that a theory explains or predicts a set of observations. In the problem-solving mode, the conceptual and empirical status of the explanatory argument merits critical analysis. "Black Box" theories—those which predict a set of outcomes given a set of inputs without specifying how or why inputs and outputs are connected—only become progressive as a theorist attempts to put substantive content into the "black box."

Deciding whether a theory solves conceptual problems involves a semantic analysis of the concepts of the theory as well as an examination of the consistency of the arguments of the theory. Communicability, empirical import, fertility, degree of specificity are conceptual properties that can be evaluated. Since I have written at some length about evaluating concepts (Cohen 1989), I will not repeat the analysis here.

To my knowledge, the question of how to decide whether or not a theory solves a practical problem has not been addressed. If the solution to the practical problem is formally derivable from the theory, then the theory obviously solves the problem. But that almost never is the case even in the highly developed sciences. Engineering applications nearly always involve extrapolations from a theory; the practical situation usually contains factors the theory ignores or treats as noise; often the practical situation is outside the scope of the theory. While derivability may be too high a standard, the requirement that the practical solution was "suggested" by the theory may not be high enough. As a provisional standard, we might require that the solution to the practical problem employ some concepts and assertions taken directly from the theory. While these concepts and assertions may not be the whole solution and may be used with other ideas, at least there is a clear linkage between the theory and the solution of the problem.

BETTER THAN OTHER SOLUTIONS?

Comparing one theory's problem solutions to other available solutions arises two types of issues: decision rules and specific criteria. Since I have assumed that the problem is an important one, decision rules are more or less straightforward. There are three cases to analyze.

Case 1. If theory T solves the problem and there are no available alternative solutions, then T is obviously provisionally acceptable and we only need to ask what T can do besides solve this problem. Those theories that cannot do anything besides solving the given problem are likely to be ignored whereas those that are progressive will eventually generate competitors.

Case 2. If T fails and there are alternative solutions to the problem, our course is also pretty clear although it differs depending on whether we are dealing with a basic research or an engineering problem. If our concern is practical application, then we should use available solutions and not pay any attention to T. If our concern is developing basic knowledge, then T's failure to solve an important problem that other theories resolve should set off an alarm and lead us to undertake more general evaluation of the viability of T. Note that I emphatically do not call for the abandonment of T even when it fails to solve an important problem for which alternative solutions exist. A more general evaluation of T may lead to abandoning T, but it also may lead to a preference for T over available alternatives.

Theorists have different thresholds for how much failure they can tolerate before abandoning a theory and that is probably a good thing. (There are many examples in the history of science where tenacity has eventually been rewarded.) Most of us would agree that T should be rejected if there were no problems for which T provided a better solution than available alternatives. In the more likely circumstance where there are some problems for which T provides the best available solutions, the failure to solve the particular problem could be ignored or it could be handled by modifying either the domain of T, or its scope or both.

I want to underscore a central tenet of the approach I am proposing: A discipline cannot afford to discard a theory that provides the best available solution to an important problem. To put it in other words, a theory with demonstrated problem-solving success has not failed; T_1 may be superceded when a better problem solver, T_2, is formulated, but even that is not failure if T_1 contributed to the development of T_2.

Case 3. The situation where T and alternatives produce equally good solutions to a given problem also calls for a more general evaluation of T along the same lines as already described. T is preferred where either it provides solutions to a range of problems that are better than available alternatives or where there is no single alternative theory that solves all the problems solved by T. In the unlikely event that there are two theories that are equivalent in both the range and quality of problem solutions, then there is no reason to prefer either theory and certainly no reason to abandon either. Of course, theories with only partially overlapping domains do not require us to choose between them. In general, we should look approvingly on the coexistence of competing or partially competing theories.

Formulating specific criteria that are comparative entails producing standards for evaluating the answers to questions like the following: Is the theory's explanation more general, more accurate, more precise, more comprehensive than available alternatives? Is the theory's logical structure clearer and/or more explicit than available alternatives? Is the practical solution drawn from the theory more efficient, less costly, more likely to be successful, less likely to produce unexpected negative side effects than available alternatives? With the possible exception of some of the dimensions in the last set, our ways for evaluating the answers to these questions are quite rudimentary; nevertheless, we can make decisions in all but the close calls. Further development of specific comparative criteria, however, should be high on the agenda of a methodology of theory construction.

Progressive Solution?

Most of the issues discussed in connection with comparative criteria are relevant to my third question, "Is the solution progressive in the sense that it opens up possibilities for solving new problems?" There are, however, some matters that pertain especially to evaluating the progressiveness of a theory. Wagner and Berger (1985) have proposed a set of analytic categories that can provide evaluative criteria. But such criteria usually require looking back at the history of the theory. Retrospective evaluation is perfectly fine for theories that have been around for a while, but we also need criteria that can be applied to the current state of a theory independent of its line of development. We recognize that it may not be possible to decide unequivocally whether a *given* theory is progressive relative to other theories with similar domains; nevertheless, there are theories for which definitive judgments can be made.

One set of specific criteria relate to the domain and the scope of a theory. Theories that can be used to solve distinct classes of empirical problems under different sets of conditions are obviously progressive. I suggest that theories with well-specified scope and domain are more likely to be progressive than those where domain and scope remain implicit. When scope and domain are explicit, it invites questions of the form, "what if we altered specification S of the scope or specification D of the domain?" The answers to such questions could lead to new problem solutions for the theory.

Considerable work is needed to develop criteria for determining the progressiveness of a theory. Without minimizing what remains to be done, let me propose one more criterion. Theories that have the capacity to confront competitors are more likely to be progressive. In part, this is outside the control of the adherents of a given theory because it depends on the existence of at least one competitor with overlapping domain and scope and that, in turns, depends on the reward system and the politics of the discipline. But this capacity also depends on the way the theory is formulated and the attitudes of its adherents. We need to formulate theories as clear challenges to existing problem solutions and we need to abandon the ego-defensiveness that attempts to protect our own theories from all challenges. While my proposal may sound utopian given our attachment to our own intellectual products, my earlier point about not abandoning theories that solve problems has implications for competition: competition among theories is not a zero sum game so that confronting a theory with its competitors could make them all progressive.

OLD CRITERIA IN NEW PACKAGING

Since much of the previous analysis sounds familiar, some critics might argue that my proposals are the same old criteria in new packaging. I suggest that while some of the elements may be similar to conventional methodology of theory construction, the overall thrust of my proposals is different. Let me summarize the key differences.

As I noted in discussing Laudan, the approach is pragmatic and internal to the discipline. It is pragmatic in its orientation to solving conceptual, empirical, and practical problems and also in its recognition that the quality of solutions is relative to what is currently available. Locating the criterion problem within the discipline is also based on the pragmatic notion that people working on problems are best able to recognize what constitutes solutions and to develop the specific criteria needed to evaluate those solutions. The emphasis of this type of methodology of theory development is down-to-earth and close to the practicing scientist rather than esoteric and limited to an initiated elite. It is not subject to the often-heard criticism of philosophy of science that the methodological injunctions ignore the successful practices of working scientists.

The second distinctive feature of these proposals is the comparative emphasis. Problem solutions are evaluated relative to available alternatives; the disciplinary context and stage of development, therefore, play central roles in evaluation process. This methodology recognizes that different stages of substantive development mandate different standards of evaluation; what is successful in an early stage of theorizing is not sufficient in later stages and what are reasonable standards at an early stage are inadequate at more advanced stages. Approaching the evaluation of a given theory or of the cognitive status of bodies of sociological theory in a comparative mode produces realistic assessments rather than a sense of frustration and futility that arises from using absolute ideals as standards.

While these criteria deal with explanation and prediction, the focus is on success rather than on failure as is the case using a falsification rule. Furthermore, since "truth" is not an issue, the approach does not attempt to infer success in general from particular successes; it does not bring "verifiability" in the back door and does not run the risk of committing the inductive fallacy. While the set of criteria draw on the work of Lakatos (1970), they avoid his troublesome notion that theoretical research programs, of necessity, have an unmodifiable "hard core," that is, a set of key assumptions that are impervious to evidence.

Many of us have discussed the idea of evaluating the confirmation status of a theory. We have done so with considerable discomfort, because we were fully aware of the difficulties of measuring confirmation status. Assessing problem-solving success is not without difficulties, but it is a more manageable task particularly since the judgments are relative and the decisions permissive. We are not asked to infer future success, but only the present standing of a theory or set of theories. We are not forced to discard one or more of a set of competing theories each of which has some success.

Moreover, relinquishing the criterion of confirmation status does not require us to give up "corrigibility." Theories are modifiable by reason and evidence if empirical research and/or logical analysis demonstrate that there are better or more progressive alternatives available. Scientists have never been as constrained as the proponents of experimental canons of inquiry would demand; they have taken negative outcomes and failures of "crucial experiments" in stride, and, Kuhnians to the contrary notwithstanding, science has progressed. Working scientists are probably more attuned to a theory's problem-solving capability than to its confirmation status, and, although methodology should lead in establishing the norms of scientific practice, in his instance methodology needs to catch up with practice.

THE CURRENT STATE OF SOCIOLOGICAL THEORY

Much of what is called sociology theory will not satisfy problem-solving criteria any more than it will satisfy traditional criteria. There is considerable confusion between metatheory and theory and there is a widespread lack of understanding of what a theory is, how a theory is constructed, how a theory is used, and so forth. Among many people "doing theory," there is not even an orientation to solving problems, conceptual, empirical, or practical. I am even willing to concede that the set of unenlightened people is larger than the set of those who are partially edified. I suspect that such a numerical distribution always prevails in any science. But a principal injunction of the methodology I am espousing is that one counts successes and ignores failures. And there are many successes so that despair is unfounded.

Clearly, I cannot provide a convincing demonstration of my claim in a short paper. At a minimum, a demonstration would entail presenting an inventory of existing theories together with a detailed evaluation of the relative merits of the solutions for the problems that each theory has successfully solved. Developing this inventory would require a lengthy study that is both extensive and intensive; needless to say, I have not conducted such a study, although I think it would be highly worthwhile to do so. However, on the basis of some unsystematic—and certainly nonrandom—observations, I am convinced that if this study were conducted, it would support my claim.

Let me share some of my observations. First of all, in the 1990s, it is not difficult to find examples of explicitly formulated theories that make researchable claims. When I entered the field in the 1950s, this was not the case; except for some formulations of the classic theorists, theory was either typology or metatheoretical polemic.

Theories that have appeared over the last three decades deal with many different substantive concerns and represent diverse subfields of the discipline. Sociologists have devised both macro and micro level theories. I have found theories which potentially could meet my criteria in what I regard as unlikely places—for example, there is a "Conflict Theory of Deviance" that lays out a series of claims in propositional form and has generated empirical research (Chambliss and Seidman 1971). I don't know if that theory continues to be developed, but it did attempt to explain a number of distinct phenomena.

Secondly, many of today's theories are closely connected to cumulative research programs and have successfully explained or predicted sets of observations. There are at least three distinct programs developing exchange theories of power (Bacharach and Lawler 1981; Cook et al. 1983; Willer 1987): resource dependence theory (Pfeffer and Salancik 1978) has generated a set of organization studies; there are emerging programs using rational choice theories (Hechter 1987) as well as a program developing a "macrosociological theory of social structure" (Blau 1989; Blau and Schwartz 1984). The program built around Expectation States Theory (Berger et al. 1974) is highly developed and has solved empirical, conceptual, and practical problems. This is by no means an exhaustive list; these are just the programs that I have had occasion to explore so I'm sure that there are others in subfields that I do not normally follow. Even if these were the only theoretically driven enterprises in the field, I think their successes would justify the view that we are making theoretical progress on a number of fronts.

My third encouraging observation is that competing theories with overlapping domains are beginning to emerge, so that it may soon be possible to make serious comparative evaluations of a theory's problem-solving ability. As I asserted earlier, conflict between competing theories is very likely to be progressive. One example of a progressive outcome occurred in the recent dispute over the concept of "vulnerability" among theorists concerned with the distribution of power in exchange networks (Cook et al. 1983; Willer 1986; Cook et al. 1986; Markovski et al. 1988; Yamagishi and Cook 1990; Markovski et al. 1990) Although my colleagues may not agree with me, I believe that the proposal of a dominance theory (Lee and Ofshe 1981) as an alternative to Status Characteristic Theory (Berger et al. 1966, 1972; Berger et al. 1977) in explaining differentiated interaction in small groups has had progressive consequences for the Expectation States Program. In these examples, progressive outcomes occurred in part because the conflicts were about the solution of empirical or conceptual problems rather than arguments about different metatheoretical presuppositions.

My fourth and final promising observation involves the self-conscious use of theory in solving practical problems. The Program for Complex Instruction at Stanford's School of Education (E. Cohen, forthcoming) has drawn on several organization theories to design a management system for heterogeneous elementary school classrooms, that is, classrooms with multiple languages and a wide range of academic achievement. In addition, treatments to mitigate status effects in these classrooms are based directly on Status Characteristic theory.

Having sketched the half-full portion of the cup, I should say something about the half-empty component. Here I have two general concerns: (1) there is a widespread lack of understanding of what a theory is and what it is not, what a theory can do and what it cannot, and (2) there are too many inhibitions against formulating alternatives to existing theories.

The lack of understanding of the nature and uses of theory unfortunately extends to many who are sympathetic to the enterprise. As a consequence of this lack of understanding, many sociologists have unrealistic expectations about what theories can accomplish and these, in turn, lead to impossible demands and/or unjustified negative assessments of theory development in sociology. For example, a person who believes that sociological theory can predict future historical events profoundly misunderstands the conditional nature of scientific theory (Cohen 1980; Walker and Cohen 1985) and is bound to be disappointed. Or a person who fails to appreciate why a theory cannot be a photographic representation of reality must be thoroughly frustrated by the necessary simplifications of any scientific theory. Or a person who holds the belief that theories deal with "wholes" rather than properties of objects will not understand the distinction between explaining the variance and theoretical explanation and also will not be sympathetic to the necessary theoretical activity of breaking down very large problems into manageable subproblems.

I have argued that assessment of theoretical development must be comparative, but I recognize that in most cases we cannot compare a theory's solution to available alternatives because there aren't any available alternatives. Because of what someone once called the sociologist's tendency to treat another person's ideas like his toothbrush, many current theories are without any competitors.

A number of features of the contemporary situation of sociology operate to inhibit the development of competing theories. The reward system puts premiums on novelty; as a result, there is little incentive to deal with problems that someone else has already considered and even less to "fix" someone else's theory. Our field pays too much homage to its ancestors so that it is more important for an idea to be faithful to the usage of some hallowed ancestor than for it to be fruitful. The fathers of our field made major contributions—I'm sure that analysis would show their theoretical work to be more progressive than that of many of their present-day disciples—but we must grow past them rather than debate the meaning of classic texts or use these to certify our own legitimacy.

Although there are probably many other aspects of contemporary sociology that work against the development of competing theories, one stands out as a particularly self-defeating characteristic. Virtually every group or school of sociologists has an inordinate concern with protecting its own turf. It becomes more important to define some other group as outside of sociology or outside of science or outside of formal theory or outside of some other artificial boundary than it is to show that one's own group can produce a better solution to a problem than the other group. We seem to get great pleasure out of showing to our own—if not to anyone else's—satisfaction that some potential rival is not legitimate.

This primitive territoriality manifests itself in endless debates over metatheory where we have shown more concern with using our ancestors as clubs than in advancing their substantive arguments. What purpose, other than turf protection, is served by debating what are social facts?

The territorial urge is at fundamental odds with a problem-solving orientation and it is ultimately self-destructive. A psychologist on an interdisciplinary panel once noted that proposal reviewers in the social sciences tended to tear apart projects submitted by their disciplinary colleagues whereas reviewers in the biological sciences tended to be very positive about projects in their own field. The result, of course, was that the biologists captured most of the grants. I think there is an important lesson here. To the extent that we indulge ourselves in parochial legitimacy battles, we risk our legitimacy with other scientists, the academic community, and the tax- or tuition-paying public. Our long-term contract with society is to increase the understanding of social phenomena; fratricidal struggles over turf impair the discipline's ability to fulfill that contract.

CONCLUSION

While I find the tendency for these turf battles to continue unabated somewhat discouraging, I am not discouraged about the state of theory development. The rate of growth may not be as rapid as I would like, but I think that whatever the actual rate, I would not be satisfied and would want it to be greater. To be sure, I would prefer that theory construction had deeper appreciation and greater acceptance in the discipline than it presently has. I don't believe we are in a golden age, but my belief is not evaluatable since historical periods are dubbed golden ages long after they are over. On the other hand, I don't think we are in a dark age either.

At the outset, I asserted that despair over the state of theory development is unwarranted. I have sketched a set of criteria that flesh out the criterion of the problem-solving capacity of a theory. By these criteria, I don't think we are doing so badly. Although I acknowledge that it would require a detailed study to support my view, I have presented examples of theories which solve empirical, conceptual and practical problems and which are progressive. We can definitely reject the proposition that such theory is impossible and, at the very least, we can conclude that the cup is not empty.

I have also considered two major obstacles to theory development, the lack of understanding of the nature of theory and the structural characteristics of sociology which inhibit the development of competing theories. A possible response to these, and other obstacles, is to be overwhelmed by a sense of futility; I think such a response is totally inappropriate because progress in constructing sociological theory does not require converting or defeating all the infields. Progress only demands that we continue to push against the obstacles, moving them back a little at a time.

The obligation of theorists is to promote the development of cumulative theory so that each new theory improves on the problem-solving ability of its predecessors. Our real enemies are satisfaction with the accomplishments of any given theory and defensiveness about the nature of our enterprise. While continually seeking to improve our theories, we also need to respond to our critics and encourage our competitors. In dealing with those who denigrate the whole enterprise, we need to abandon the Kuhnian copout of incommensurability and ask them what problems they have solved lately. In dealing with other theorists, we need to give up the attitude of "You go to your church, I'll go to mine," the attitude of benign indifference, and actively seek ways for theories to confront one another.

The proportion of sociologists involved in theory development is small and will probably always be small. We can rail about that state of affairs, but such complaining is counterproductive. I am reminded of what Adlai Stevenson said in eulogizing Eleanor Roosevelt, "She would rather light a candle than curse the darkness." It's time we lit a candle.

Notes

1. Note that this is different from saying that we ought to formulate true theories.

2. By calling theories, "instruments," I do not want to get involved in the realism-nominalism controversy; both "realist" and "nominalist" theories need to meet the test of successful problem-solving.

Part 2
Alternative Strategies for Developing Formal Theory

A variety of theoretical strategies exists in sociology. Perhaps the best listing of the many different ones current in sociology is provided in the beginning of the Collins and Waller paper (chapter 1). They observe that some want theory closely tied to empirical work, others even advocate laboratory experiments so that causal inference is more sound, while still others believe in a division of labor between theorists and empiricists as exists in physics. Middle range is still another strategy but one that some argue against (see chapter 9 and Turner's comments in the concluding part). But these strategies are quite independent of what is the ultimate object, namely the view of what formal theory is.

The words "formal theory" can even produce some debate and disagreement as a comparison of the opening of Cohen's essay with that of Gibbs' (first paper in this part). Cohen believes that the terms of formal theory deny the process of theory building, which includes formalization. He wonders what informal theory is. One answer is provided in Gibbs' lament about the discursive mode. Generally, however, the term "formal theory" is an acceptable label for most of the other contributors.

What went largely unnoticed at the conference in Maryland was a change in vocabulary. Twenty years ago, the emphasis in the various books that were published was on *theory construction*. At the conference these words were seldom mentioned; the discussion focused on formal theory. The shift in terms is probably all to the good. The real objective of the theory construction movement was formal theory and perhaps this should be the crux of the debate, not how one constructs formal theory.

But what is formal theory? Both Gibbs and Cohen agree about what is perhaps the most critical element of a formal theory, namely what the former calls predictive power and the latter problem-solving effectiveness. This criterion relates directly to the issue of building status for the discipline and generating job opportunities in both the nonacademic and academic world—presumably the more of the former, then the more of the latter.

Implicit or explicit in each of the chapters in the first part have been alternative models of what formal theory is. Turner most explicitly argues against the model used in physics and instead suggests that the best model is the one employed in biology, particularly in evolutionary theory. What he means by "physics envy" is an emphasis on axiomatic or deductive theory. In contrast, Hage explicitly argues for this very approach in chapter 9, where a number of examples are provided to show how an emphasis on assumptions and scope conditions might help build bridges between the fragmented parts of the discipline, a fragmentation which Turner also deplores. Abell (chapter 6) in his contribution also suggests that we should emphasize deductive theorizing as does Chafetz (chapter 8). This has been the avowed strategy of the Stanford research program and thus reflects the preference of Cohen (chapter 4).

But while Turner and Hage might disagree about deductive theory, they can agree that evolutionary theory might confront the more fundamental question or strategic theoretical site and thus the more useful focus for sociological theory. Not only is there an issue of whether formal theory is helpful in advancing the field, and what is meant by formal theory, but there is also a consideration of which theoretical areas might lead to the biggest intellectual gain. Evolutionary theory might be one. In chapter 9, Hage suggests that society's changes across time make some paradigms more important and even provides some examples of how action laws might be postulated about this evolutionary process.

Where Hage and Abell disagree is the subject matter of the formal theory. Abell believes that we should emphasize interactive processes with formal game analogues, starting with the micro level and building upwards. Thus, his approach is very similar to the program of Coleman (1990). In contrast, Hage is explicitly arguing for the inclusion of premises or assumptions from different kinds of specialties, regardless of whether they are from the micro or the macro level, and preferably both. Both however do agree about the need for boldness.

Blalock and Hage share the view that the complexity of social reality is not being captured and that too much attention is being paid to the principle of parsimony. Hage's solution is to combine assumptions from different paradigms with an emphasis on scope conditions, which automatically increase the complexity of thought. Thesis and antithesis are combined. In contrast, Blalock emphasizes such ideas as nonlinear relationships and feedback processes, relationships that are generally ignored in the theoretical literature. These kinds of connections between ideas would also make our theories not only more complex but also more dynamic, the lack of complexity and dynamism being a common failing of most theoretical work to date.

Another area of agreement that appears to exist, yet is hidden by lexical differences, is the need for formal theory to focus on process. Certainly, this seems implied in Turner's (chapter 2) call for a model of theory similar to the work of Darwin. Hage's action laws (chapter 9) appears to be similar even though these exist in physics as well. In particular, Hage in his discussion of role theory versus symbolic interactionism touches upon evolutionary theory and one that relates micro and macro levels. Abell is also concerned about a theory of process, one that clearly recognizes sequences, while he stresses his preference for the micro level. Process is also implied in the examples from Chafetz's level. Finally, Blalock by stressing feedback processes, offers a methodological approach to the problem of process. Here is one topic that probably deserves much more attention and discussion than it received at the conference. Has sociology failed to develop because it has not given enough attention to processes and especially evolutionary processes?

Consensus also existed about the importance of connecting empirical data with theory. In his analysis of the disjuncture between theory and research in England, Abell (chapter 6) advocates their being coupled. Blalock (chapter 7) is the most explicit on this point as he considers the kind of methodological problems that are presented when joining theory and research. All of the various chapters that deplore the fragmentation are implicitly suggesting the need for the joining of theory and methodology in the view of formal theory.

Chafetz (chapter 8) specifically focuses on the defects in most theory courses; the courses are not problem oriented, yet is problem-solving which inevitably makes one appreciate the connection between theory and research; this is the same point made by Cohen when he discusses problem-solving capacity.

Both Chafetz and Hage in their respective contributions look at particular substantive areas where formal theory might be usefully applied. Chafetz emphasizes the importance of developing formal feminist theory, while Hage in his discussion of mobilized classes and strong states touches upon an area that has generally been ignored, that is, the mobilization of women, and instead focuses on classes, especially the working class as the main protagonist. In contrast, in his example of role theory, Hage recognizes some of the important work of feminists who have examined textbooks used in schools to indicate how role theory is critical to a feminist agenda.

In part 3, the concluding chapter, Turner also argues for a substantive attack that he labels grand theory, that is theory that attempts to put together the entire field or at least large sections of it. He believes that some scholars—if not all—must attempt this strategy of developing grand theory so that the field may advance. Merton once said, it at least makes for fruitful errors! Abell (chapter 6) appears to agree with Turner when he wants to focus on fundamental social processes and games that describe interaction sequences. And while Hage (chapter 9) does not discuss grand theory, he supports the idea that synthesizing basic assumptions from different paradigms should lead to some kind of grand theory.

Another issue that should be debated in the discipline is perhaps best stated as a question. How much formalization should there be? Turner (chapter 2) argues that the theory construction movement overemphasized formalization, which is probably an accurate criticism. But then the question remains as to the degree of formalization; the latter comes by incremental stages. There might be more consensus in the field on some medium position that is in-between discursive language and a completely symbolic language or mathematical language, as has been advocated by Cohen (1985). Does one want to avoid the statement of assumptions or premises in a formal way? I think not, but then this is for each reader to decide.

5

Resistance in Sociology to Formal Theory Construction

Jack P. Gibbs

Within seven years following the 1965 publication of Zetterberg's *On Theory and Verification in Sociology,* sociologists published eight books on the methodology of theory construction.[1] All nine books, including Zetterberg's proposed at least a partially formal mode of theory construction, something quite different from the conventional mode. There is no basis to argue that Zetterberg's book was the trigger; but whatever prompted the authors, the general reaction of other sociologists is now obvious. Few sociologists came to use a formal mode of theory construction, and the publication of books on the subject virtually ceased.[2] For that matter, the nine books did not alter assessments of well-known sociological theories, meaning that sociologists continued to venerate the works of deceased Europeans.

Although some of the nine authors (e.g., Gibbs 1972, v–vi) were not optimistic, few of them anticipated any particular resistance to formal theory construction; and even today the major sources of that resistance have not been identified.[3] Their identification is this chapter's paramount purpose, but there is a more distant goal. At least a few sociologists are convinced that their field will remain third-rate as long as the conventional mode of theory construction prevails; hence, they should take this question seriously: How can resistance to formal theory construction be overcome?

BRIEF CLARIFICATION OF KEY TERMS

Although sociologists ostensibly revel in debates that center on ill-defined notions, those debates are inherently sterile. So it is desirable to define each of this paper's four key terms, even though space limitations preclude a defense of the definitions.

90

Methodology of Theory Construction

Defined all too briefly, the methodology of theory construction is the analysis of problems and issues concerning alternative forms and procedures for *stating* theories. Such methodology is metatheoretical in that it transcends particular theories. To illustrate with a prescription: In stating a sociological theory, the rules of deduction must be made explicit. Surely that prescription transcends particular theories, and it bears on the form of theories rather than their substance.

Even the term "methodology" suggests a source of resistance to formal theory construction. Any formal mode is methodological, and students are best introduced to contending modes in a methodology course. However, just as numerous sociologists complain that sociological methodology is dominated by a concern with quantification to the neglect of qualitative methods, so is that dominance a source of resistance to formal theory construction. Such is the case because statistics or mathematics cannot be equated with formal theory construction, even granting that in the case of a theory encompassing quantitative variables the *ultimate* goal is the expression of at least the theorems in the form of equations.

A Mode of Theory Construction

This term denotes nothing more or less than a set of rules to be followed in stating a theory. Even the person who formulated the rules may regard them as incomplete, but the distinction between a complete mode and a partial mode is conceptually irrelevant.

Complete or incomplete, no mode of theory construction constitutes a *logic of discovery.* Any mode presupposes the ideas that are to be expressed when stating a theory, and no mode gives directions for generating those ideas. Recognition of that point may be a source of resistance to a concern with formal theory construction; specifically, the criticism or unexpressed misgiving will be that formal theory construction does not meet the real need. Therefore, advocates of formal theory construction should argue emphatically that even the possibility of a logic of discovery is dubious, especially without using the term "logic" uncritically.

The Discursive Mode of Theory Construction

This term designates the conventions of some natural languages, such as English or French, as the set of rules to be followed in stating a theory. A more elaborate definition is scarcely needed, because virtually all sociological theories were stated in accordance with the discursive mode. Hence, if the pejorative character of the label "discursive" is objectionable, it can be replaced with the label "conventional."

The argument can be supported readily by reference to the theories of Durkheim, Marx, Pareto, Simmel, and Weber. Those theories exemplify the use of the discursive mode. What do we find when we examine the form of those theories? Virtually all of their constituent parts are ordinary sentences and paragraphs, with no labels to distinguish them as to type or position in the theory. In the few instances where a grand theorist did apply some label to a sentence—such as postulate, proposition, or hypothesis—the label is puzzling not only because bereft of a rationale but also because such labels are alien to the conventions of any natural language.

So the veneration by sociologists of classical or "grand" theory is a major source of resistance to formal theory construction. It is as though each generation is socialized so as to accept this admonition: What was good enough for Emile, Karl, Vilfredo, Georg, and Max is good enough for you. Accordingly, to promote formal theory construction, its advocates should never tire of criticizing the *form* of grand theories, whatever an advocate may think about the *content* of those theories.

A Formal Mode of Theory Construction

A mode of theory construction is formal if and only if at least *one* of its constituent rules was formulated expressly to be used in stating a theory, meaning that the rule is not a convention of some natural language. Here is an illustration of such a rule: *Any* statement that is deduced from a theory's premises must be labeled a "theorem." Would anyone seriously argue that the rule is a convention of the English language?

The illustration is apt when opposing a widespread belief, one that equates formal theory construction and the use of mathematics in stating a theory. To be sure, the language of mathematics is not a natural language; but in stating a theory "mathematical sociologists" appear to presume that the use of equations need not be preceded by a *formal* verbal statement of the premises (axioms, postulates, and/or propositions) and conclusions (theorems). Thus, Coleman's colossal version of rational choice theory (1990) bristles with equations; and yet the *form* of the verbal articulation is conventional (i.e., discursive), scarcely different from the form of Parsons' action theory.

There is no dominant formal mode of theory construction in sociology; rather, there are several contending modes, but none widely used. The problems created by that divergence are examined subsequently, and at this point one argument will suffice. It is a mistake to assume that resistance to formal theory construction is limited to particular modes of versions.[4] It is likely that most sociologists resist formal theory construction *in general,* and that resistance is fueled primarily by an attachment to the discursive mode. Hence, advocates of formal theory construction should do more than promote a particular mode; they should never tire of criticizing the discursive mode, for they can agree appreciably in those criticisms.

INHERENT ADVANTAGES AND DISADVANTAGES

One major source of resistance of formal theory construction can be described very briefly: natural language conventions are more flexible than are the rules of any formal mode of theory construction. To illustrate, natural language conventions do not require recognition of parts of a theory other than sentences and paragraphs, let alone labeling parts as to type. By contrast, a formal mode *may* call for some of a theory's component statements to be labeled as definitions, some as procedural prescriptions, and some as empirical generalizations, with each generalization labeled as an axiom, postulate, proposition, or theorem. Such explicit labeling is a far cry from mere ritual. If nothing else, it serves to clarify the theory's logical structure, and it promotes recognition of the distinction between testable and untestable statements. However, explicit labels for parts of a theory require decisions that need not be made when using a natural language, and for that reason alone a theorist may view a formal mode as a burden.

Terminological Considerations

The discursive-formal distinction has no bearing on sociology's substantive terminology. Whether stated discursively or formally, a sociological theory comprises terms so technical that they are scarcely components of a natural language; but most of those terms are *substantive* in that they denote entities or properties of entities, with six examples being: society, community, class conflict, anomie, cohesion, and suicide rate.

No formal mode prescribes *or* proscribes the use of any particular substantive term; but, for reasons indicated later, a formal mode is incomplete unless it *prescribes* the use of particular "relational" terms to the exclusion of all others. Thus, a formal mode may stipulate that only one of two terms, "varies directly with" or "varies inversely with," is to be used when asserting a relation between quantitative variables. There is no such stipulation in natural language conventions, and the alternative relational terms are so numerous that an unrealistically short illustrative list for the English language must suffice: based on, causes, is associated with, gives rise to, determines, is sufficient for, depends on, follows, essential for, found with, results in, and increases with.

Should someone try to duck the problem of terminological diversity by arguing that most of the terms are synonyms and can be so identified readily, he/she is blissfully ignorant of ambiguities in the English language. Yet the diversity and ambiguities of relational terms in a natural language makes it much easier for a theorist to use that language than a formal language, and greater flexibility is not the only consideration. If only because of the theorist's prior mastery of a natural language, he/she is not likely to relish learning a formal language. Indeed, although theorists who use the discursive mode are not necessarily lazy, a lazy theorist is least likely to abandon that mode.

The Disadvantages of a Natural Language

The diversity of natural language relational terms gives a theorist an enormous range of choices, and there is nothing to prevent him/her from deliberately selecting a term with an especially ambiguous meaning. Thus, rather than appear incredulous when asserting that variable X causes variable Y, the theorist may assert that Y is "based on" X, thereby virtually insuring a debate over relevant evidence. The illustration is unrealistic only in suggesting that the term "causes" has a fairly clear meaning and, hence, can be used without creating problems.

The general argument is very simple. In a natural language the relational terms are so diverse and ambiguous that their use when stating an empirical generalization virtually precludes defensible tests of the generalization, meaning congruence in reports of tests by independent researchers pertaining to the same events or things. Moreover, a theory is never stated as one isolated empirical generalization, and a sociological theory is likely to be such that *some* of its constituent empirical generalizations are not directly testable. Evidence can be brought to bear on such an empirical generalization only if it is a premise and enters into the deduction of at least one testable prediction. Defensible deductions are precluded when the logical structure of the theory is obscure, but sociologists are not prone to recognize that a theory's logical structure is likely to be unclear if the theory has been stated discursively. Sociologists are imperceptive because their criterion of a clear logical structure may be little more than this: If the theory is comprehensible, then its logical structure is clear. To bring evidence to bear on premises that are not directly testable, a much more stringent criterion is imperative. A theory's logical structure is sufficiently clear only when independent observers agree in identifying the theory's premises and as to what statements are implied by those premises.

The logical structure of the typical sociological theory is not sufficiently clear if judged in light of the stringent criterion. There are a numerous passages in sociological theories that end with a sentence having an initial phrase something like this: "It follows from the foregoing that. . ." (see illustrations from the literature compiled in Gibbs 1972, 102–6). The phrase suggests that the conclusion has been deduced; but inspection commonly reveals that the conclusion cannot be deduced by any rules known to logicians, or known to sociologists for that matter.

The suggestion is not that sociologists need only adopt conventional rules of deduction. No formal mode is complete unless it prescribes deduction rules; but as long as sociologists feel free to use the relational terms of a natural language when stating a theory, conventional rules of deduction cannot be applied to the premises. Stated otherwise, prescribing the use of particular relational terms *to the exclusion* of all others is necessary for rigorous rules of deduction. Should that claim be doubted, confront this question: How can it be argued that the terminology and deduction rules of the classical syllogism, Boolean logic, mathematics, or even the "sign rule" are natural language conventions?

The Crucial Question

So why do sociologists cling to the discursive mode? One answer is simple: any formal mode is perceived by most sociologists as a burdensome constraint. However, advocates of formal theory construction should emphasize another answer: the discursive mode of theory construction prevails because its critics have not made sustained and coordinated efforts to force recognition by all sociologists of the mode's disadvantages.

The disadvantages of natural languages are by no means limited to the bewildering variety of relational terms; but that variety alone precludes rigorous deductions from the premises of a discursive theory, even presuming that the premises can be identified with confidence. So advocates of formal theory construction should focus on that defect because it is especially crippling. Of course, they are reluctant to launch a full-scale attack because they recognize that discursive theories may be interesting and offer insights, but where is sociology today after more than a century of dominance by the discursive mode of theory construction?

THE PREDICTIVE POWER OF THEORIES

The primary rationale for formal theory construction is that a theory's predictive power cannot be assessed defensibly if the theory was stated discursively. Hence, the least conspicuous source of resistance in sociology to formal theory construction[5] is widespread indifference if not hostility to assessing theories solely in terms of predictive power.

Evidence of Indifference If Not Hostility

All manner of difficulties preclude even an estimate of the extent to which sociologists accept or reject predictive power as the basis for assessing theories. So a few general observations must suffice.

Throughout the field's history, sociologists have displayed an astonishing tolerance of untestable theories. Indeed, given the veneration in sociology of grand theories and the common indifference of sociologists to the few testable theories in their field, sociologists clearly pay little attention to testability when assessing theories. Nonetheless, because a test is nothing more or less than the falsification or corroboration of a prediction derived from a theory, testability is a dimension of predictive power. True, all of the predictions implied by a theory may prove to be false, but that possibility pertains to a quite different dimension of a theory's predictive power—predictive accuracy.

Sociologists are evidently reluctant to express their indifference or hostility to predictive power, and that reluctance conceals a crippling dissensus in the field. Nonetheless, numerous commentaries on the way that sociologists assess theories are relevant. Consider, for example, Gouldner's claim (1970, 30) that sociologists regard a theory as intuitively convincing because it confirms their background assumptions. Gouldner did not acknowledge that sociologists may oppose a theory because the theory does *not* confirm their background assumptions, and there was no suggestion whatever by Gouldner that sociology faces a crisis because sociologists assess theories without reference to predictive power.

There is abundant evidence of alternatives in sociology to predictive power as a basis for assessing theories. Thus, Alexander (1982, 1983) creates the impression that theories are to be assessed by examining their underlying "presuppositions," something that has no necessary connection whatever with predictive power. Then Weber's disciples demand that theories promote understanding, and they insist that there is no connection between understanding and accurate predictions.[6] Finally, humanists in sociology never tire of warning their colleagues against taking physics as the model of science; and in the few cryptic comments that have been made about an alternative model, the notion of predictive power is ignored entirely.

The Ascendance of Antipositivism and Ideology

A conspicuous increase in antipositivism commenced in sociology some twenty-five years ago, and sociological theories came to be assessed even less in terms of their predictive power. The significance of the change will not be appreciated without recognition of the primary rationale for formal theory construction. Again, a theory's predictive power cannot be assessed defensibly unless the theory is stated formally. Once the rationale is recognized, one can see why antipositivism promotes indifference if not hostility to formal theory construction. So the timing of the nine books on the methodology of theory construction was a disaster; and formal theory construction faces a grim future as long as sociology is gripped by antipositivism, even though over recent years the term "positivism" has become little more than a pejorative label.[7] The typical usage is like a dog barking in the night; it suggests aggressiveness, but the target is not known.

Positivism is defined here as nothing more or less than the insistence that scientific theories should be assessed solely in terms of predictive power. However, insofar as antipositivists even suggest a definition of positivism, it is often something like this: positivism is the belief that science is, can, or should be value-free. Hence, antipositivists are prone to promote the value-laden view of science but without acknowledging this corollary: Acceptance or rejection of a theory should be based on a judgment of the values (or ideology) that the theory supposedly furthers and not on the theory's predictive power.

The counterargument is not that theories are value-free in every sense; rather, sociologists will never realize even effective consensus in assessing theories if their assessments are implicitly or explicitly based on ideological criteria rather than predictive power. In any case, the ascendancy of antipositivism in sociology has worked against formal theory construction, because antipositivism stems from a determination to accept or reject theories for reasons that have nothing whatever to do with predictive power. Consequently, it is not puzzling that many sociologists embraced Kuhn's arguments (1970) enthusiastically despite his doubts about the applicability of those arguments to the social sciences.

Kuhn's work demonstrates that the ascendence of antipositivism was not limited to sociology; but it also demonstrates the seeming reluctance of antipositivists, whatever their field, to answer this question: What *should be* the primary if not exclusive criterion for assessing the merits of scientific theories? That question is paramount for any science, but dodging it has become an art form in sociology. The most recent dodge is Burawoy's focus (1990, 775) on "What should we mean by science?" without ever formulating an explicit definition of science, let along identifying the criterion that should be used to assess scientific theories. Buraway's ostensible alternative—invoking Lakatos (1978)—is a dodge because an instance of Lakatos' "research programs" may be partially based on or reflect an explicit or implicit criterion for assessing theories, but in itself it is not a criterion. Indeed, if it is argued that a research program can be the criterion, the immediate question is: What program? The general point is that Lakatos' arguments about research programs do not answer what is identified here (*supra*) as the paramount question, let alone are they such as to circumvent or resolve the related issues.

Before the Ascendancy of Antipositivism

Prior to the late 1960s it was difficult to identify the genesis of hostility in sociology to the idea of assessing theories in terms of predictive power, but even before the ascendance of antipositivism there was nothing like effective consensus as to appropriate criteria for assessing theories. In particular, Par-

sons' brand of sociology (see, especially, Parsons 1951) discouraged acceptance of predictive power more than has the shrillest version of "critical
sociology."

It could be that antipositivism always has stemmed in part from a mis-
understanding of the very notion of predictive power. Many sociologists evidently equate the terms "predictive accuracy" and "predictive power,"
meaning that they recognize only one dimension of predictive power. Accordingly, they are inclined to construe an emphasis on predictive power as in-
dicative of bareface empiricism, and that interpretation might persist even if
it were made clear that a theory's predictive accuracy is to be judged relative
to that of contenders rather than by some absolute standard, let alone a physical science standard.

Some Dimensions of Predictive Power

For reasons just suggested, antipositivism might be lessened should sociologists come to recognize that there are several dimensions of predictive power
other than predictive accuracy. Space limitations preclude more than a very
brief description of three of the six other dimensions: scope, range, and
parsimony.

Scope is the most conventional, and it can be described simply as the
number of dependent variables in the theory. However, despite the simplicity
of the notion, it is an illusion to suppose that independent observers can agree
in describing the scope of a discursively stated sociological theory, especially
of the classical or grand theories.

Each variable in a theory pertains to a property of some type of unit; and
sociologists work with an astonishing variety of types, such as families, organizations, age groups, cities, occupations, and countries. So if two theories purport to explain variation *only* in the suicide rate, both would have
minimum *scope;* but their *ranges* could be quite different. If one of the theories purports to explain variation in the suicide rate only among, say, age
groups, its range would be at a minimum and only one-third that of a theory
which purports to explain variation in the rate among, say, age groups, occupations, and countries. Sociological is an unusual science in that the notion
of range (so defined) has less relevance for various other fields. Nonetheless,
the range of the typical sociology theory is obscure because there are no rules
in the discursive mode that govern the use of terms that denote types of units.

Finally, *parsimony* can be assessed in terms of the ratio of the number of
conclusions (theorems) in a theory to the number of premises. Any other criterion makes it virtually impossible for independent critics to agree when
comparing particular theories; but the criterion can be applied (if at all) to
discursively stated theories only with great difficulty, because of uncertainty
in attempts to identify premises and conclusions.

The suggestion is not that a formal mode somehow insures greater parsimony, scope, or range. If there is a difference, discursively stated theories have a greater scope and range than do formally stated theories; and the contrast is so great as to suggest an inherent advantage of the discursive mode. But discursively stated theories have a greater scope and range because the discursive mode enables the theorist to leave the logical interrelations of the constituent statements obscure, and there is a rarely recognized consequence. Definitions of a scientific theory (see Gibbs' survey, 1990) commonly require that the parts of a theory be logically interrelated, and the requirement raises doubts about the status of all discursively stated theories in sociology. Be that as it may, one source of resistance to formal theory construction is that it makes it more difficult to create the impression, when stating a theory, of having realized enormous scope and range.

DIVERGENT FORMAL MODES

Still another source of resistance in sociology to formal theory construction is the divergence of contending formal modes. A detailed description of that divergence would require a very lengthy paper; hence, the present treatment of the subject must be very general and all too brief.

Some Illustrative Contrasts

Some of the contending modes are much more elaborate than others in that they comprise more rules and related distinctions. As a case in point, all of the modes clearly indicate that statements are the basic components of a theory, because words, terms, or phrases by themselves are not necessarily meaningful communications; but only a few of the modes explicitly prescribe the use of particular rules of deduction. The contending modes differ also when it comes to recognition of major divisions or parts of a theory. Thus, only some modes emphasize the need for a clear-cut separation and labeling of two major categories of statements. One of the two categories comprises definitions or analytical statements but also possibly procedural stipulations, such as formulas and instructions pertaining to requisite data; and the other category comprises empirical generalizations or synthetic statements.

What should a mode of formal theory construction comprise? It may well be that there is not a great deal of agreement in answers, not even in answers by advocates of formal theory construction; and reliable inferences cannot be drawn from the contending modes, because a mode's author may not have intended to formulate a complete mode. For that matter, some of the nine books in question (i.e., Blalock and other authors cited in endnote 1.) were written as a treatise on both substantive theory and the methodology of theory construction. Yet even the articulation of one rule for stating a theory constitutes a partial mode of formal theory construction if the rule is not merely a natural language convention. To be sure, at least for certain purposes it would be desirable to treat the "formality" of a mode of theory construction or a particular theory as a matter of degree, but that subject is far too complex for an examination in this chapter.

Some Illustrative Issues

All contending formal modes of theory construction recognize types of empirical generalizations; unfortunately, however, there is little agreement as to the types, meaning that there is nothing like a uniform use of such labels as axiom, postulate, proposition, theorem, and hypothesis. Even when two modes use the same label to designate a particular type of statement, the definition or rationale for the label may be quite different.

Such contrasts are not surprising because there are at least two bases for typification of statements—the statement's position in the theory or the nature of the statement's constituent terms. Although most modes recognize that a theorem is derived from premises, there is little agreement as to types of premises, ostensibly because of divergent ideas about the kinds of constituent terms that should be distinguished.

Perhaps the most important divergence pertains to relational terms. For example, some modes prescribe covariational terms, such as "varies directly with" and "varies inversely with," while others prescribe a causal language.[8] The contrast makes divergent deduction rules inevitable. Indeed, it may be that a mode stipulates no deduction rules precisely because the mode's prescribed or implied relational terms make it difficult to formulate rules.

TWO PATHS TO GREATER UNITY

This paper stops short of passing judgment on the contending formal modes of theory construction. Their divergence harms the cause of formal theory construction, but agreement on one mode can be realized only through collaborative efforts. Although the most effective way to organize such efforts is debatable, there are two paths to greater unity among advocates of formal theory construction.

Focus on the Defects of the
Discursive Mode

Reconsider a previous question? What should a formal mode of theory construction comprise? The answer could come in two parts, the first being: A formal mode of theory construction should comprise whatever is needed to avoid the defects of the discursive mode. One illustration must suffice. Sociologists who use the discursive mode uncritically assume that natural language conventions are sufficient for rigorous deductions. Consequently, there is a compelling argument for regarding a formal mode of theory construction as grossly incomplete unless it prescribes deduction rules.

Unfortunately, two advocates of formal theory construction are not likely to agree about the appropriate rules of deduction without prior agreement as to the appropriate relational terms for empirical generalizations, and there is every reason to suppose that some advocates of formal theory construction will argue for causal terms and others for covariational terms. Both arguments have real merits.[9] So perhaps at least in the short-run two modes of theory construction are needed, one in which the relational terms are causal and the other in which they are covariational.

The strategy would not lead to a proliferation of alternative modes if advocates of formal theory construction focus on avoiding the defects of the discursive mode, but a mode for stating *qualitative* theories is needed. If such a mode is formulated but not used by those sociologists who complain about the predominance of quantitative methodology, it will indicate that the quantitative-qualitative distinction conceals the real issue—whether theories are to be assessed by reference to their predictive power. Similarly, advocates of formal theory construction must expect persistent opposition from sociologists who promote the "humanistic" perspective and are at best skeptical about the very idea of a "scientific" sociology. Unfortunately, not everyone who endorses that idea are enthusiastic abut formal theory construction, but "scientific" sociologists in general and advocates of formal theory construction in particular are sensitive to a question that humanists never confront. Entirely apart from invidious comparisons, how does sociology differ from investigative journalism, theology, history, social work, philosophy, and social criticism?

The Second Path to Unity

Again returning to a previous question: What should a formal mode of theory construction comprise? The second part of the answer to the question is this: A formal mode should comprise whatever rules and related distinctions are needed to facilitate the assessment of a theory by reference to all dimensions of predictive power. One illustration must suffice. Consider a rule that requires an explicit unit term (e.g., countries, age groups, cities within a multiracial country) in each of the empirical generalizations that are components of a theory. The rationale is that explicit and consistent unit terms reduce ambiguity, thereby enhancing testability; and they facilitate assessment of the theory's range—the greater the variety of unit terms, the greater the theory's range.

A focus on dimensions of predictive power would do more than promote unity among advocates of formal theory construction. Again, it may well be that many sociologists resist formal theory construction primarily because they believe that it is conducive to a preoccupation with predictive accuracy and leads to bareface empiricism. Hence, a formal mode of theory construction should make it obvious that predictive accuracy is only one of several dimensions of predictive power.

To conclude, sociologists will not adopt formal theory construction unless they become thoroughly dissatisfied with rhetoric as the primary medium for defending and criticizing theories. That consideration is all the more important because even though most sociologists are not incorrigible ideologues, they appear to crave polemics. That craving makes them especially vulnerable to the appeals made by advocates of critical sociology, deconstructionism, emancipatory sociology, French structuralism, hermeneutics, liberating sociology, Marxist semiotics, postempiricism, postmodernism, postpositivism, poststructuralism, and so on, ad nauseam. Yet rhetoric has no real bearing on predictive power,[10] and it does not mix well with formal theory construction. So, as long as sociologists are swayed by rhetoric rather than by tests, by predictive accuracy, and by other dimensions of predictive power, theorists will cling to the discursive mode of theory construction, because that mode is indispensable for rhetoric. Indeed, to end with a depressing prophecy, as long as the discursive mode of theory construction prevails in sociology, the field will remain little more than a debating club; and the debates will become even more monotonous.

Notes

1. Blalock (1969), Dubin (1969, 1978), Gibbs (1972), Hage (1972), Mullins (1971), Reynolds (1971), Stinchcombe (originally printed in 1968 and reprinted in 1989), and Willer (1967).

2. Since 1972, Chafetz's book (1978) and Cohen's (1989) are two of the very few signs of continued interest in formal modes of theory construction, at least in the sense of this paper's definition of that term. Of course, there is long tradition of sociological books focused on substantive theory as much as if not more than the methodology of theory construction (e.g., Freese 1980, Gross 1959, and Turner 1989), and that description extends even to some of the nine books in question (especially Stinchcombe 1968). Moreover, sociologists are prone to use the term "metatheoretical" in connection with *substantive* issues (e.g., conflict vs. consensus) rather than in connection solely with methodology.

3. Documentation of resistance is difficult if only because there is no extensive critique of formal theory construction in the sociological literature. Criticisms are largely limited to casual remarks in conversations, commentaries by anonymous journal referees, and statements in book reviews (see, e.g., *Contemporary Sociology* 19:866).

4. It is no less a mistake to assume that sociologists need look only to the philosophy of science for a formal mode of theory construction. Insofar as a formal mode can be used by all of the sciences, it fails to come to grips with problems that haunt theory construction in some particular sciences much more than others (e.g., because sociology borrowed so many of its terms from the humanities, where they were defined vaguely if at all, sociology has terminological problems far greater than physics ever faced). So it is pointless to presume that a mode of theory construction appropriate for the physical sciences can be used effectively by sociologists. However, humanists in sociology notwithstanding, it does not follow that *criteria for assessing the merits of theories* cannot be the same for all sciences.

5. Another inconspicuous source of resistance is the ostensible belief by some sociologists that formal theory construction is pretentious. That belief is recognized here in a note because it deserves no more attention than this:

the best way to reveal the possible pretentiousness of a discursive theory is to restate it formally.

6. Dubin (1978) argues as though there can be no connection between sense of understanding and predictive accuracy; but imagine a theorist saying something like this: my theory makes it possible to make consistently correct predictions not only as regards variation in the suicide rate but also individual differences (i.e., victims vs. nonvictims); yet I understand nothing whatever about suicide. The more immediate point is that Dubin's stance alone creates doubts about the extent to which advocates of formal theory construction are prepared to assess theories in terms of predictive power.

7. As demonstrated by Halfpenny's survey (1982), long before the ascendancy of antipositivism the term "positivism" had so many different meanings (at least twelve) that it was unfit for purposes of scientific communication, critiques in particular.

8. Compare Dubin (1969, 1978) or Gibbs (1972) with Blalock (1969).

9. Unfortunately, both of the two alternatives have what critics regard as major shortcomings. If the mode of theory construction permits only premises that assert covariational relations, the temporal quantifiers of the variables may be such as to suggest causation (see Gibbs 1972); but the theorist's conception of causation is left implicit. On the other hand, if the mode requires that the theory's premises assert causation, defensible tests of the theory are precluded unless the mode comprises rules for deducing "covariational" theorems from "causal" premises. Most modes stop far short of stipulating or even suggesting such rules, and the rules stipulated or suggested by the exceptions (e.g., Blalock 1969) are ambiguous and/or grossly incomplete. Moreover, there is no prospect of defensible rules until sociologists abandon their ostensible reluctance to confront problems and issues pertaining to the notion of causation (for elaboration, see Gibbs 1982).

10. If theories are to be assessed in terms of predictive power or simply "empirical validity," what is gained when a theorist convinces the audience to accept the theory through persuasive arguments that have nothing to do with test findings (predictive accuracy) or other dimensions of predictive power? Such a "hard sell" is merely a personal triumph, and it promotes indifference to the need for testable theories and systematic tests. Indeed, if theories are to be assessed in terms of appeals to preconceptions, presuppositions, or background assumptions, why even devote lip service to the need for tests?

6

Sociological Theory: What Has Gone Wrong and How To Put It Right, A View from Britain.

Peter Abell

The two most renowned contemporary British sociologists are John Gold-thorpe and Anthony Giddens, and in different ways their work represents the undoubted achievements of British sociology. But on inspecting their writings closely, one cannot fail to notice a remarkable fact. Goldthorpe seems able to address the empirical problems he chooses to study with only the most cursory reference to the theoretical traditions with which Giddens deals, and furthermore, Giddens' most recent writings seems to be less and less constrained by the demands of empirical research. Why should this be so? Should we worry about it? And if we should, is there anything we can do about it?

I think we should worry, for the manifest reason that theoretical traditions which fail to engage empirical research are ultimately doomed to sterility, and in the first part of this chapter I will try to determine why this strange division has arisen. In the second part, I will turn to what we might do about it, by making a case for a revamped approach to sociological theory which stresses the need to deductively model complex many-actor strategic systems which are often coupled together in remarkably intricate ways. I foresee, however, little chance of achievement in this respect without placing some reliance upon formalisms. Indeed, I shall argue that the gap between theory and empirical research can only be closed in this manner.

WHAT WENT WRONG?

Contemporary British sociology is largely shaped by the consequences of the dramatic expansion in the number of sociologists employed in the universities in the late sixties and early seventies. The people who entered the discipline at that time now hold the key posts, increasingly control the journals, and dictate the intellectual climate. They have, individually and collectively, achieved much. Most of the major universities and polytechnics now possess a flourishing sociology department, and though the discipline has experienced a number of vicissitudes, its standing both in the public eye and in academe, while not high, is probably more secure than it has even been.

The sociological profession was, though, gaining ground in a period of unprecedented postwar social and political turmoil, when it was almost mandatory for the aspiring sociologist (often a refugee from other disciplines) to offer cogent critical comment upon the significant movements of the time. It was not a period for instance, when painstaking technical analyses could easily flourish. The mood was too impatient for that; big statements about big issues were called for, and big philosophies were invoked. Though there was to be disillusionment and an eventual retreat into micro interactionism, this again was not to prove fallow ground for the formalist. At least not for the received potential formal orthodoxies, which depended either upon statistical techniques or upon a rather crude importation of natural science models (e.g., an emphasis upon differential and difference equations).

Furthermore, those who entered the discipline in such large numbers and on such a compressed time scale sought to construct sociology using those intellectual skills which were most readily at their disposal. Even those hailing from disciplines which offered a grounding in formal analysis were to turn their backs on these skills, often taking a principled stand against what they saw as inappropriate incursions of positivism. All this proved to be particularly true of those who sought to promote theory which increasingly attracted great prestige. Although, historically speaking, the much vaunted empirical tradition in British Sociology, going back for several decades, was there to be grasped, its intellectual standing was also beginning to take a buffeting at the hands of increasingly strident attacks on 'positivism' deriving from the Continent. Indeed, just when a number of North American sociologists, who were to dominate the discipline a decade or so later, were on the verge of making the most significant contribution to empirical sociology which had been made for years, by importing and adapting econometric-type modeling into mainline sociology, the swelling ranks of British sociologists were increasingly discounting the significance of anything of this sort. This had two consequences: first, theoretical approaches which had as little intellectual contact as possible with the burgeoning formally based empirical techniques were sought; and secondly, nonformal empirical procedures (often qualitative methods of one sort of another, for these until recently, were largely innocent of any formalism) were strongly promoted. It is, I think, rather significant that despite the long-standing empirical tradition in British sociology, going back to the beginning of the century, there has not been a single major British contributor to the establishment of the generalized linear model (path modeling) as a major research framework. The drama of British sociology over the last two decades is to be found elsewhere, and comes with a sometimes explicit but more often than not implicit, rejection of any suspicion that sociology is the sort of discipline which is in need of an appropriate formalism. This rejection has had a particularly marked and deleterious impact upon the development of sociological theory. A few have stood out against the trend, but they have in effect been marginalized.

There are many ways in which one could instance the consequences of these unhappy developments, the most damaging, however, is the prevailing conception of sociological theory which encourages a never-ending debate about the nature of theory itself. Theory becomes a reflexive exercise rather than one substantially directed towards empirical puzzles. Theoreticians characteristically refer to one another and refine conceptual tools rather than construct deductive models. Theory is embedded in philosophy and rarely, if ever, finds the energy to propose isolated, let alone deductively related, propositions. Furthermore, there is scant evidence that it is of much use to those who do try to take this path. Indeed some, including Giddens, have chosen to write of social as opposed to sociological theory—perhaps, in part, in recognition of this state of affairs.

Though one cannot deny the importance of paying some attention to the epistemological issues which lie at the foundations of any discipline, there are clear limits to what is worthwhile. Contemporary sociological/social theory (not only in Britain) has, in practice, become suffused by the untenable assumption that significant intellectual advances will only be secured when any foundational conceptual problems have all been cleared up, allowing a fresh start to be made. This is, of course, a misplaced idea, coming from those more steeped in analytical philosophy than scientific practice. The history of intellectual life in disciplines other than sociology prove it to be a false assumption and there is no good reason to suppose our discipline is likely to prove significantly different. Advances are, in practice, secured by making conceptual compromises in the rough and tumble attempt to parsimoniously capture the complexity of real world mechanisms. The art of science is to be found in knowing what to discard, in judging what to ignore, and in rejecting the incursion of rampant epistemology.

As soon as one begins to address empirical puzzles which are at all problematic (i.e., those which necessitate a theoretical solution), it rapidly becomes evident that we are dealing with mechanisms which are of such complexity that is often not easy to see how they can be approached without resort to some sort of formalism. In my view, it is difficult to conceive of a sociological theory of any real intellectual depth which is not to some degree formally based, if only because formalisms show us how to render complexity in a systematic manner. No doubt this conclusion is colored by the conception I hold of what theory should be designed to achieve, something which will, I hope, become clearer below. I should say here, though, that I exclude from my strictures what we might term descriptive theory; that is to say, the formulation of more or less abstract descriptors of social reality, whatever that might be deemed to be. Much "theory" is of course directed this way and it would be absurd to make my above claims in respect of this activity, but surely we should ask more from our theories than this. Indeed, I would argue that descriptive theory of this sort should be formulated in a manner which invites deductive subsumption.

British sociological theoreticians have taken a tack which has given us the disjunction I noted in opening, between the contributions of Goldthorpe and Giddens and, on present practices, never the twain shall meet. Goldthorpe will continue his largely empirically led studies and Giddens will pour forth more "theory" which will have no decisive impact upon empirical study. We have, if sociological theory is to have an appreciable impact upon empirical research, to reshape it, but this will be no easy matter. Before theory can become relevant to the best social research, it needs to find securer foundations in deductive modeling. For this to be accomplished, the appropriate formalisms need to be located and then mobilized. In my view, the teaching of sociological theory will have to be radically altered in order to promote the inculcation of the appropriate skills. Unfortunately, I see little prospect of this happening on a significant scale in Britain, the entrenched interests in continuing with more of what we already have are just too strong. Nevertheless, it is worth sketching what might be involved, though since I wrote the first version of this chapter we have been blessed by the publication of two books (not in Britain) which take us a quantum leap in the right direction; namely Coleman's *Foundations of Social Theory* (1990) and Fararo's *The Meaning of General Theoretical Sociology* (1989). These dwarf anything I have to say.

GENERATING THEORY

I shall seek in the rest of this chapter to promote what I shall term reasoned interaction and belief theory (RIBT) as the most promising framework for the development of a genuine propositional sociological theory. This objective will, however, be approached indirectly as my first purpose is to defend the notion that sociological theory should take on a deductive appearance. But why so? After all, the doyen of British theorists has urged against such a perspective, or, at least, against "theory . . . expressible as a set of deductively related laws or generalisations" (Giddens 1984). While it is probably unwise to speak of laws—perhaps quite frequently of generalisations also (I shall return to the notion of generalisation)—I shall argue, contra Giddens, that deductive modeling is the only way to construct a sociological theory of any depth which is at the same time empirically useful.

The answer to the above question is, I think, rather obvious. We wish, as sociologists, to theorize about complex many-actor systems with structured patterns of interdependence (often of a strategic variety, though Coleman, [1990] has strongly promoted nonstrategic exchange models) which generate consequences which are sometimes intended and foreseen by the actors concerned and sometimes not. *The complexity of these (strategically) structured systems is such that the only prospect of modeling them is by making bold axiomatic assumptions, deducing consequences, and testing these against experience.* But, as we shall see, it is important to pay attention to the nature of the 'language of experience.'

In order, however, to head off a possible misinterpretation, it must be said that this emphasis upon deductive modeling should not be taken to imply that the inductive assembly of empirical "facts" has no role to play in the scheme of things. Indeed, such assembly, in either variable-centered or account-centered format (Abell 1987) is more often than not a prompt for a deductive model. Patterns of covariation of ethnographically generated patterns may invite the formulation of a model purporting to show how they are strategically generated by the reasoned interactions and beliefs of the individuals or sometimes collectivities.

It is important to underscore the central role which should be afforded to the concept of *strategic interdependence* in sociological theorizing. It merely means, there exists between some or all actors, reciprocal beliefs/ expectations about each others past, present, or future likely courses of action as a consequence of their interdependence (i.e., their joint determination of what happens or outcomes). Parsons, of course, in his 1937 vintage propounded a similar view, although it unfortunately led him to a taxonomic rather than a propositional view of sociological theory. It is worth noting here though that if actors are not strategically interdependent (or at least one dependent on another) then the need for a sociological theory is to a significant degree undermined. I take it that "interactionists" would endorse this statement. When actors act or forebear to act independently of each other, then there is nothing specifically sociological about this—sociological theory is not to be constructed out of the aggregation of independent exogenously determined actions. The same point can also be made in respect of the generative mechanisms behind those beliefs, values, and socialized affects which go into actions (are constitutive of actions). Once again, the need for sociological theories of these mechanisms arises, in contrast to individual learning theories, because of strategic interdependencies in the learning (socialization) processes themselves. I think these points are often lost sight of, with the consequence that sociological theory is then made to look like aggregate social psychology or the simple aggregation of constitutively exogenous individual actions. This, it seems to me, is to miss the sociological point. It does not follow though that aggregate phenomena are devoid of sociological interest (e.g., the consequences of n people voting entirely independently of each other). It only follows that there is not a theoretical problem which relates exogenously given actions to outcomes with which the sociologist may engage.

From this perspective one, if not the, central theoretical issues for sociological theorists may be described as the structured aggregation problem. How do individual actions/interactions combine to produce social (macro) outcomes as a consequence of the actors strategic interdependencies? (Coleman 1990; Boudon 1981).

Since the proper subject matter of sociological theories are strategically structured many-actor systems, the appropriate formal framework may prove to be "games in networks". That is to say, the appropriate formal vocabularies for a genuine theory may well be found with game theory and network analysis (Fararo and Skvoretz 1981). At least this appears to be the most promising avenue open to us at the moment. I am not so sanguine as to believe that game theory is currently developed in a form which we, as sociologists, can immediately embrace; Elster's (1989) recent experience should dissuade us of this view. However, a start should be made in this direction and certainly courses in sociological theory should afford a grounding in utility and game theories.

The argument for a deductive perspective on theory does not derive from either positivist aspirations or from its aesthetic appeal. It is simply that there is no serious alternative. Indeed, the reason why much contemporary sociological theory is so unsatisfactory is precisely because it has failed to take this lesson to heart. Rather than tussling with the technically demanding job of modeling complex strategic systems, sociological theorists have either lapsed into metatheory or served up lists of more or less isolated propositions. Both of these latter activities have their place, but if they drive out the former, then there is little hope that theory will have any deep impact upon empirical research.

It is, I think, important to be clear about what is worthy of the name theory and what is not. In a discipline like sociology, there seems to be natural tendency to treat all problems "theoretically" and as a consequence to rapidly reach for abstract nouns which apparently give a theoretical gloss to what might otherwise appear rather pedestrian. There is no doubt that renaming things is an important activity, and adopting a fertile conceptual framework is a clear prerequisite for any serious theoretical model building. What is more, there is no warrant for an assumption of a theoretically neutral observational vocabulary; in this sense, everything is theoretical. There is and always will be a role for the sort of theory which generates interesting sets of "factual" observations—albeit theoretically laden ones. The relationship of this sort of theorizing to the making of generalizations is well understood and needs no rehearsal here. For instance, the classic relationship between the social-economic status or SES of parents and their children is clearly dependent upon a prior theorization of SES. But SES enters social mobility (occupational achievement) models in a manner which might be described as following the precepts of "descriptive theory." The point to be made about this sort of theorizing is that if the relationships once established are in some sense transparent or obvious to us, then there is no call for a deeper conception of theory. The answers to our queries are provided by an appeal to the "facts" and this is all there is to it. Significant theoretical problems arise when such facts are puzzling and are socially constructed (intentionally or otherwise) be strategically structured multiple-actor systems. So the facts engineer a demand for deductive theorizing—we need to know how the actors involved, in their myriad interactions, "make" patterns of covariation or distributions.

Because the intellectual horizon of much theorizing has been of the "descriptive" variety, a dangerous tendency has arisen for rampant neologizing which carries little conviction, particularly for lay readers of sociology. Pretentious vocabulary takes the place of hard thought and we wind up with all the disadvantages of a technical vocabulary and none of the advantages.

There is another sense in which the word "theory" is used and which should in my view be handled with some care. I refer here to what one might term sociohistorical extrapolation. For instance, Daniel Bell's Post Industrial Society is often described as theory thereof. Nevertheless, however ingenious the weaving together of trends is, in this sort of work, we should resist the designation theory in any deep sense. This is because many of the trends and their causal interconnections demand a theoretical explication in the sense I am advocating it here. And bestowing the accolade theory tends to cut off this deeper sort of theoretical inquiry.

I shall in the balance of this chapter be preoccupied with establishing how a deductive framework adequate to the modeling of complex strategic interactions may be approached. But there are a few other points which go along with the framework which ought to be mentioned. First, the complexity of strategically structures systems is such that one must be prepared initially to take many factors as exogenous. This of course goes against the grain, certainly in functionalist circles, where it often appears as though the aspiration is to explain everything at once. This is, in practice, a recipe for triviality. It is, of course, imperative to introduce exogenous assumptions clearly and explicitly to that they can be relaxed in a systematic way as one's theoretical confidence and grasp grows. The technical demands of finding partial equilibrium solutions are probably beyond us at the moment let alone general equilibrium ones.

Second, if what I have had to say in the preceding paragraphs has any truth attached to it, then one might quite legitimately ask why there is not more evidence of attempts to construct deductive models of the sort that I am advocating. For even despite the antiformalist bias I have described, one would have expected some attempts of this sort and, if my argument is anywhere near correct, some of these should have by now proved their worth and became established. This does not seem to have happened, not only in Britain but everywhere else also. I might be ill informed but it is my impression that very little formal/deductive theory has penetrated mainline theory anywhere in the world and this must be regarded as surprising if my arguments have any virtue whatsoever.

It might be helpful to look at an example of formal theorizing which, while based upon discursive theory, has failed to impress the sociological profession sufficiently to get it established as a going concern. Simon's formalization (1957) of Homans' (1950) theory of group interaction is a case in point. Why is this not an established bit of theory? Why is it that, even though Homans' original nonformal version of the theory gets onto reading lists, Simon's apparently much more powerful version (deductively speaking) does not? Surely we cannot merely put this down to an antiformal bias? Things must go deeper than that. It will be recalled that Simon sets up a series of linear time-dependent equations in variables like "intensity of interaction" and "sentiments of friendship" and deduces, within a comparative statics framework, various equilibrium conditions. These go well beyond Homans' original version and one might have though they would have been received with acclaim in theoretical circles. Certainly, Homans' original theory goes little beyond what I have termed descriptive theory and it is only with Simon's elaboration that we encounter any theoretical depth. Simon's theoretical formulation would permit us, if we were so disposed, to calibrate a set of parameters concerning the relationship between the variables involved and then to use these to explore the equilibrium characteristics of the model. Surely this is precisely what good sociological theory should do! But as far as I am aware, nobody has thought it worthwhile to take up this challenge. I suspect the reason to be that few of us really believe in our heart of hearts that any estimated parameters would show the sort of retest stability which is required of theoretically significant parameters. That is to say, the relationship between variables like "frequency of interaction" and levels of "interpersonal friendship" would not be stable nor usefully comparable across groups or "styles" of interaction. Simon provides an ordinal (monotonic) interpretation of Homans' theory, but this is predictively too weak.

The conclusion we should perhaps draw is that "theory" is not going to look like this at all. In attempting to formulate theories in the manner in which Simon does, one is forced to adopt such a thin descriptive phenomenology of the social world (i.e., simple scaler variables) that any derived parameters are inherently unstable. To put it another way, the initial conditions (interaction conditions in terms of Simon's linear additive models) are so complex that it is unlikely that they could be instanced in a way which would stabilize parameters in a population of correspondingly reduced scope. Rather than resort to a thin phenomenology we must find ways of deductively modeling thick description (often in natural language format). In practice, human interactions take the form: A does X, which leads B to do Y, etc. Where X and Y stand for complex descriptions. In effect, Simon has in some way to reduce this sort of complex sequential structure to simple counts of one sort or another. A more promising approach, in my view, is to find a modeling framework which can accommodate the sequence in something like its full descriptive richness as the explanandum. Our theories should then show how sequences are generated and, in the case under review, produce sentiments of friendship (as in unintended outcome). For example, although formulated in a rather restricted context, Axelrod's (1984) analysis of "tit-for-tat" in the iterated prisòner's dilemma (PD) is a much more fertile approach to theory construction. There we witness, as I advocated above, a multiple-actor system generating a sequence of interactions.

Fararo and Skvoretz (1981) and Fararo (1989) have made use of production systems and finite automata to study the generation of sequences, while Abbott (1984, 1986) has developed methods for systematically comparing sequences themselves. These seem to offer promising formal frameworks for the development of theories. But in my view the most useful approach is to interpret sequences as derivable from games of one sort or another; that is to say, either as repeated strategies in supergames or as moves in games in extended form, often with incomplete information. In this way strategic thinking takes up a central position in our conceptualization (Abell 1991). More or less extended sequences of actions become the explananda which find their explanans furnished in terms of the games being played. I would include here also normatively generated sequences (Schotter 1981). Although it is difficult to find any reasonable alternative to this program, we must be open to the possibility that some sequences are of such complexity that there is not prospect at all of theoretically accounting for them. We can then only provide a thick phenomonology (Elster 1989). Although, rich descriptions of this sort are, as I have noted, inherently theoretically laden, I do think it is important to resist the temptation to get involved in renaming things in terms of abstract "theoretical" typologies which do not derive from an understanding of the complex reasoned interactions which underpin them. There is no justification for creating equivalence classes which are not underpinned in this way.

THE FOUNDATIONS OF REASONED ACTION AND BELIEF THEORY

It might in many circumstances be entirely proper to interpret RIBT as rational action or choice theory, but the idea of rationality is sometimes used so restrictively that it is better to use the term *reasoned*. This allows space for subjective rationality and does not tie one to the axiomatics of objective rationality, though such might often be the first resort of the model-builder—or at least some well-authenticated adaptation like prospect theory (Khaneman and Tversky 1979). Expressed most generally, RIBT assumes the features of the social world which invite theoretical explanation (often predescribed in descriptive theoretical terms) are generated by strategically reasoned interdependent human actions. What I shall term the starting paradigm runs as follows:

1. Specify the outcome one wishes to explain: this may be an event (the storming of the Bastille), a state of affairs (an income distribution), or a covariation (the correlation between children and parents SES). It may be expressed in variable or account centered format. It may be unique, thus inviting a singular explanation, or it may be a general phenomenon inviting a general explanation.

2. Specify the actors involved in the generation of the outcome. These may be individuals or collectivities of one sort or another. The special problems of dealing with collectivities fall beyond the scope of this essay (but see Abell 1989).

3. Specify the cognitive/information/knowledge environments of the actors. This is essential since reasoned interaction is dependent upon both the information and modes of reasoning available to the actors. What are sometimes called complete/full information rational-choice models are thus to be seen as rather special cases of the starting paradigm.

4. Assume the goals/objectives/preferences/utility functions of the actors.

5. Assume the resources available to each actor; these may be very variable and quite subtle.

6. Model the structure of the actors interdependencies (i.e., how outcomes are jointly dependent on their actions).

7. Deduce the consequences of (2) to (6) and test against (1).

Note that four important "variables" are taken as exogenous in this formulation—the cognitive information environment, the goals of the actors, the structure of interdependencies, and the distribution of resources. A later challenge is to make some or all of these endogenous. At the moment they may often be regarded as an omnibus criterion of "social position" as conceived by structuralists. Indeed, as Elster urges in numerous places, "structural determination" can be viewed as a special case of this sort of paradigm where the possibility/feasibility set is reduced to a single action, though the actors presumably could still forebear to act and, on this count, the word determination might be a misnomer. Furthermore, the nature of strategic interdependence of actors may determine a unique equilibrium (in one of the many game-theoretic senses of this term) and consequently will hold the promise of a theory of rational determination. In the absence of such, or in the presence of multiple equilibria, additional axioms will be needed to render the theory determinate. The theoretical interest of a sociological problem arises very largely because of the intricacies involved in modeling the way in which, firstly, local strategies emerge as a consequence of interdependencies and, secondly, how these combine to produce collective or macro outcomes. Indeed, as noted above, if outcomes are generated by the independent aggregate actions/forebearances of actors then there is little of theoretical interest to detain us—at least as sociologists. In my view, the most pressing need for the would-be theoretical sociologists, is the formulation of a general approach to how actions and forebearances which are locally strategically reasoned get combined into macro outcomes (Coleman 1990). Theoretically underanalyzed examples of this general problem abound in classical sociology. For instance, the way in which, in the Marxian conception of class, individual action is translated into collective action. I would at this point have liked to provide such an approach but this has proved beyond me. All I can do here, is outline some of the salient issues at stake.

It is clear that the revival of interest in exchange theory is of great significance, for most patterns of interdependence can ultimately be reduced to exchanges of either alienable or inalienable assets of one sort or another. The structuring of actions through power, authority, and bargaining (cooperative or noncooperative) are, of course, central, and though much has been written by sociological theorists about these concepts, it has by and large been innocent of the technical literature. In addition, interdependencies generated by externalities include the provision of public and club goods will provide a focus for the theory builder. This is particularly so in the fabrication of norms, conventions and institutions (Ullman-Marglit 1977; Schotter 1981). Since the preferences, opportunities, information environments, and interdependencies are given (exogenous), the starting paradigm will normally define a game, usually of incomplete information. The various issues which arise, therefore, art not unnaturally those derived from a game-theoretic perspective. They are:

116   *Abell*

1. How many players are involved? And if there are a relatively large number, can the game(s) be reduced to ego versus the rest? If so, this very considerably reduces the complexity of the modeling.

2. Are the games zero or variable sum? If they are the latter, are the games of pure cooperation or not? In either case, are they played cooperatively or not?

3. In practice, the paradigm will only in special circumstances yield a unique *n*-actor game as actors will be involved in more than one game either concurrently or sequentially (e.g., a production game with externalities and a bargaining game in work organizations). Sociological theorists will have to master the art of modeling systems of multiple games with intricate interconnections.

4. Patterns of interdependence may be complete, strongly or weakly, connected or unconnected. Concepts derived from network analysis like structural and regular equivalence will in all probability prove useful in modeling ideas of structural position (Fararo 1990). They will provide a picture of who is strategically related to whom. The theory of graph restricted games is in its infancy (Myerson 1977; Owen 1986) but holds promise.

5. Simple 'contact structures' like diffusion and ecological models might provide a baseline where inter-actor interdependencies are minimally strategic, if strategic at all. Here, no game is involved, but the dynamics are structurally shaped. Competitive market exchange models are, of course, nonstrategic (net of assumed respect of property rights and at least some basic trust and/or sanctioned enforcement) and, thus, will not normally reflect the complexity of strategically structured social systems. The starting paradigm accordingly is not an invitation to incorporate the precepts parametric exchanges into sociological theorizing. It should, however, be noted that much of Coleman's (1990) recent theoretical work operates with assumptions of parametrically given values in exchanges of one sort or another.

6. There are, of course, a number of attempts in the literature to use games in normal form to model social systems. They, however, ultimately lack conviction, even though they often help in tidying up conceptual issues (e.g., Elster 1989). In my view, this is for two reasons—both of which can, to a considerable degree, be remedied. First, the games are usually reduced to simple binary choices (e.g., cooperate or not in prisoners' dilemma and chicken) when degrees of cooperation are possible. Second, there is an underuse of games in extensive form. Most strategic systems are highly complex in the sense that a given strategy (i.e., a game in normal form) is constituted out of many moves, and, this being the case, the extensive version of a game is often the more appropriate modeling framework. Indeed, as I have argued earlier, the appropriate explicandum in sociological modeling is usually a sequence of actions/interactions and, thus, sequence analysis (Ab-

bott 1990; Fararo 1989), comparative narratives (Abell 1987), and event structure analysis (Heise 1988) will provide the most telling frameworks. The purpose of theory is to deduce these from the complex and often interactive games that generate them. I will now attempt to set out how this purpose might be achieved.

Few, I suspect, would wish to deny that the social world is comprised of highly complex networks (partially ordered in time) of interrelated actions and forebearances (i.e., interactions). Much 'descriptive social theory' is devoted to the intricate problems of describing (conceptualizing) this world and, from differing intellectual perspectives, the actors involved may be individual persons or social collectivities of one sort or another. I do not wish here, however, to get involved in the debates about the relative virtues of methodological individualism and collectivism, so I will, merely for expository purposes, simply adopt an individualistic perspective.

Given the assumption that the social world is a network of some sort or another, then the key question becomes one of how to construct optimal conceptual interventions. We may further assume that the 'art' of doing so is one of *only* locating sufficient descriptive detail to effect comparisons and, thus, to locate any inherent generalizations (i.e., general mechanisms). Once we are armed with a knowledge of the array of these mechanisms, we may then study how they combine in complex ways to generate the ongoing networks of social life. My hunch is (and it is little more than that at the moment) that the best way of securing these twin objectives is, as I have intimated above, to adopt a framework which combines a rather general approach to strategy (i.e., games) and to networks.

It may help at this stage to revert to the Homans-Simon model introduced earlier, to see what might be involved. Let us assume, for illustrative purposes only, that the world is comprised of a single type of simple strategic mechanism, namely a binary prisoner's dilemma (PD). (This is not, in fact, quite as absurd as it might seem, as it can be convincingly argued that all exchanges with an inter-temporal component rest upon a PD.) Thus, individuals repeatedly engage in simple binary PDs (cf. Axelrod). Now the Simon intervention in this world would follow the precepts of standard (positivist!) social research; that is to say, the invocation of the variable centered method and all it implies (Abell 1987). It would have us search for a covariation between the *number* of cooperative interactions (encounters) and the emergence of bilateral amity. This is all very fine, of course, if it stands up and by that we must mean that it enables us to detect a generalized pattern of (statistical) determination. This, as I suggested above, has not (and is unlikely to?) prove to be the case. It is instructive to see why; an analysis of the underlying issues, is, I think, extremely revealing. In adopting the language of variables and statistical/causal determination (the standard language of much empirical research) as one's basic descriptive vocabulary , one in general thins the phenomenology, but in particular, abstracts away from the strategic nature of the interactions. The explicandum is the relationship between the number of cooperative interactions and the level of friendship. The first-order explanans is the corresponding generalization (circumscribed by appropriate initial conditions—i.e., interaction conditions). Strategic issues can, of course, be incorporated into the picture, but only as the axioms of a second-order explanans. Three steps up the explanatory tree, as it were. I repeat, if it works, then no doubt this is the optimal theoretical/empirical research intervention available to us. It certainly has proven its worth in much of those parts of economics where strategic models are used. Axiomatic assumptions are made about patterns of strategic interactions, from which propositions about variable states of the world are deduced, and then these are tested against experience. Why not build upon this approach, keeping the strategic vocabulary entirely for the explanans? Why is it not the case that the 'optimal intervention' in social networks is likely to take this form?

Let us return to Simon. One way of answering these questions is to see what is *lost*, in our simple world of PD interactions, by adopting the variable-centered (Simon) method. First and foremost, in concentrating upon a count of interactions (or even a proportion of cooperative ones) *the sequence of the interactions is lost*. Thus, for instance, a count with an underlying tit-for-tat strategy (Axelrod) would not be distinguished from an identical count with an entirely different strategic structure (see Axelrod 1984 for possibilities). Putting it another way, the *order* of the interactions in time is not considered to be of empirical/theoretical significance (Abbott 1989). This is because the strategic component of the interactions is stripped from the explicandum in the use of a simple variable-centred vocabulary. Such stripping is, though, only optimal under rather special circumstances, and only then can strategic considerations be confined to the explanans. This is so to the degree that: (*a*) there are many cases (circumstances) where the variables potentially co-vary, and (*b*) the mechanisms connecting them are relatively *uniform* and *simple*. In these circumstances we can and should feel obliged to let the explanans do the strategic modeling (e.g., use classical deductive modeling in a positivistic framework). To the degree that they are not (and I suspect this often is the case in social systems), then a thicker phenomenology must be preserved in the explicandum. It is precisely here that richer descriptions of the sequence of actions which connect earlier and later events must be retained. In this respect, if no other, then we have lessons to learn from descriptive theory, particularly that of an interactionist type.

Let us finally push the Homons-Simon example a little further. Now assume that the social world is not only comprised of sequential binary PDs, but in addition, there are also sequential bargaining games going on. The latter could be viewed as bargaining over the fruits of cooperation in the PD game. The mechanisms which might connect the count of interactions and consequent amity are now neither uniform nor simple. Indeed, it may prove impossible to consider the PD and bargaining games in analytical isolation, as they will probably *interact*, in the sense that the outcome of a bargaining encounter will effect the outcome of a PD encounter, and vice versa. The moves in the two games will also be temporarily intercalated. It seems unlikely that anything of interest will emerge by resorting to an explicandum of counts. Most of the strategic interrelationships between the games will have to be preserved in the complex narrative which goes on. When comparing one such system with another, then the narratives themselves will have to be compared (Abell 1987). Useful theories are generated when complex 'facts' are found—narrative studies and sequences are such facts.

If sociological theory is reconstructed along these lines, then there is some considerable chance that it may come to inform and guide empirical research. If it is not, then I see little future for it. There is scant prospect, however, of any reconstruction taking place in Britain: the interests embodied and reproduced in the established intellectual culture are, unfortunately, probably too strong. It will have to happen elsewhere.

Note

I have benefited from a reading of an earlier version of this paper by Stephen Hill. He greatly disliked it, but nevertheless made many constructive suggestions. I would like to thank him.

7

Why Have We Failed To Systematize Reality's Complexities?

Hubert M. Blalock, Jr.

Nearly all sociologists give lip service to the notion that social reality is highly complex. Yet we seem to prefer relatively simple theoretical explanations of this reality, together with data analyses and measurement-error assumptions that are also highly simplistic. Why is this so, and what are the implications of sidestepping theoretical and methodological complications in terms of knowledge accumulation in the discipline? I believe that there are a host of exceedingly important questions we need to ask if, indeed, sociology is to advance very far beyond its present confused state.

Before turning to the theoretical side, let me simply note that very few empirical researchers pay serious attention to the *methodological* literature, which contains numerous warnings about methodological traps and artifacts that, if ignored, are likely to produce highly misleading interpretations resulting from poor measurement, faulty research designs that needlessly confound the impacts of intercorrelated independent variables, the neglect of casual feedback loops and the overreliance on recursive models, the neglect of nonlinear and nonadditive relationships, and a host of other problems. Over the course of my own forty-year experience in the field, I have been far more impressed by the tendency of researchers to follow the latest methodological fad than to face the much broader range of methodological issues that, from time to time, have been raised and then promptly forgotten by practitioners.

I mention this phenomenon because I do not believe that the concerns being addressed by the present conference are in some way peculiar or that we can be safe in assuming that once problems and issues have been addressed by a small group of concerned theorists, the implications of what we may agree on will automatically filter through to the larger body of sociologists. My ma-

121

jor concern for the discipline is basically that I believe we are not attracting enough high-quality researchers *or* theorists, that there is far too little focus to our collective efforts, and that the overwhelming majority of our profession simply do not want to hear the bad news!

In my view, the bad news is that since reality is indeed complex, so must be *both* our theories and our research. Simple theories may be useful for polemic purposes or to motivate policy-oriented research, but my experience has been that they either explain such a small percentage of the variance that the tendency is to make too much of weak findings or that their explanatory power overlaps considerably with that of "rival" or alternative theories. In either case, the result is a series of unresolved disputes in which the proponents of different orientations talk past one another and group themselves into one or another "schools" of thought that typically exclude the variables used by those adhering to other theoretical traditions. We hang onto our favorite independent or explanatory variables, almost regardless of their success in accounting for empirical relationships.

What, for example, would a Marxist or conflict theory of drug addiction look like? It would tend to place almost the entire blame for the phenomenon on capitalistic systems, invoke notions such as worker alienation, and look for high concentrations of drug use among the "underclass," the homeless, the unemployed, and so forth. Drug use in socialist countries would be conveniently ignored. Use by members of the elite would be blamed on competitive tensions and perhaps a "basic alienation" from self or work produced by a capitalistic system. Perhaps this is a mere caricature of conflict theories, which would undoubtedly contain considerably more jargon, but I have seen enough explanatory theories of this sort to expect some such boiled-down version would be tested empirically and found to explain perhaps five percent of the variance in drug usage. I just recently read a well conceived and well executed MA thesis "testing" a conflict theory explanation by predicting a nonlinear relationship between class position and several measures of criminal behavior, with the prediction that serious crimes would be concentrated among the so-called underclass. The author indeed found that his nonlinear model explained twice as much variance as did a linear one—two percent instead of one percent.

Some of our difficulties in this connection stem from data availability problems. Usually, one can dredge up five or six control variables as well as a few rather obvious independent variables that pad the explanatory power of the entire set. There are obvious sex and age differences in the perpetration of violent crimes. Age at marriage and marriage duration work rather well in explaining fertility. Once such obvious variables have been controlled, however, the remainder don't do nearly as well. Multiple correlations of .3 to .4 (representing 9 to 16 per cent explained variance) are considered substantial.

At the macro level, intercorrelations among variables linked to development and industrialization are usually so high that one can select liberally among them to "account for" other development-related variables such as average literacy levels or per-capita GNP. Temporal sequences being nearly impossible to pin down, investigators are then likely either to remain at the descriptive level or to invoke their favored explanatory variable(s), ignoring altogether complications produced by multicollinearity, hypersensitivity to measurement error, aggregation biases, biases in ratio variables produced by underenumeration (Long 1980), and a host of other methodological complications. Alternative theoretical explanations work almost equally well, although slight alterations in measurements or research design may tip the balance in favor of one or another of the theories (Gordon 1968).

The unpopular message I wish to convey in the remainder of this chapter is that *both* the development of systematic theory *and* the kinds of data analyses needed to test such theories will require considerably more thought, resources, cooperation, and patience than the vast majority of sociologists are willing to produce or endure. I believe that the basic reasons are similar to those behind the general neglect of systematic theory development, and I will have more to say about them in the final section. In order to produce lasting changes in the intellectual products we are attempting to develop, I believe we must, first of all, attract a much higher proportion of theoretically inclined and methodologically trained students, and we must also drastically alter the normative climate and publication standards of our discipline. The problem, as I see it, therefore goes well beyond the need to produce more systematic theory since, were it available to those willing to make the considerable effort to study it, my diagnosis is that it would still be ignored by the vast majority of our profession.

WHAT KIND OF SYSTEMATIC THEORY?

There have been many different kinds of approaches to theory construction, as well as audiences to which our arguments have been addressed. My own approach has been directed primarily toward quantitatively inclined empiricists, who for the most part have tended to ignore the fact that any kind of interpretation of substantive results must invariably involve a set of *a priori* assumptions, which may either remain implicit or, preferably, can be brought out into the open for public scrutiny. For example, common practice is to ignore the fact that the true disturbance terms produced by omitted variables cannot be correlated with any of the independent variables in their respective equations.

I have preferred causal modeling and structural-equation approaches because of the fact that a variety of complexities can be handled in such a way that variables with low explanatory power can be dropped while others are added. This type of approach is distinct from more formal mathematical modeling, which generally uses a very much smaller subset of variables and highly restrictive assumptions, though with the attractive features of entailing a much simpler but more elegant set of mathematical equations with greater deductive power. No doubt a variety of formal or systematic theoretical approaches need to be tried and somehow melded together, and so I would by no means try to argue in favor of a single mode of attack, at least not until one or another has proved far more successful than thus far seems apparent.

Why direct one's arguments toward empirical researchers, rather than those who prefer to call themselves "theorists?" I believe that systematic theorizing, or indeed any other form of theorizing, must address itself to questions that, at least in principle, can be stated in rejectable form and that therefore can be modified on the basis of empirical evidence, rather than persuasiveness, ideological or value preferences, or fad. This point of view seems to be generally accepted in the profession, though my own observation is that "theorists" tend to talk primarily to each other, rather than to the bulk of empirical investigators. There is a danger, then, that those who prefer one or another brand of mathematical modeling will form a highly restricted network, as will those who are primarily interested in historical interpretations of macro phenomena or those who primarily follow the exchange theory orientation, and so forth. In my judgment, our modeling tools or methods of formalization need to be much more eclectic in the sense that they can not only handle a variety of empirical phenomena and kinds of variables, but that they can also incorporate complexities of many different kinds, as the need to do so arises. Furthermore, our theoretical tools must be comprehensible to the overwhelming proportion of sociologists who lack the mathematical backgrounds to cope with most kinds of stochastic models, simultaneous differential or difference equations, and the like.

Of more fundamental importance is the fact that relatively simple theories, when put to the test, often turn out to explain or account for relatively small percentages of the variance in whatever dependent variables we wish to investigate. If so, there is the danger of premature simplification through which considerable efforts are made to formalize theoretical arguments that are basically very weak in terms of empirically based criteria. To be sure, the arguments advanced may be elegant and perhaps even expressed in terms of sophisticated mathematical models. Concepts may be carefully defined, with axioms distinguished from theorems and assumptions made reasonably explicit. The really critical assumptions, however, may concern the operation of omitted variables, of which there are likely to be a very substantial number. Needless to say, the greater the variance "explained" by such omitted variables, and the larger the percentage of such variables are completely unknown to the theorist, the less plausible one's *ceteris paribus* assumptions become.

Simple mathematical models also will contain "constants" or parameters that are taken as givens in the case of any one data set but that are likely to become variables once the domain of inquiry or one's scope conditions have been expanded. But if such constants are indeed variables, then these need to be explained in their own right, and this will add complexity to the equation system. If the more complex system, in turn, contains "constants" which must also be explained, what was originally a rather simple mathematical model will become increasingly complex.

Parameters, if they are to be given substantive interpretations, must also be named, with important implications for the substantive interpretations given to each of the equations in the system. Consider, for example, the parameters in any one of Richardson's (1960) arms race differential equations. If we examine only the level of arms in the first nation, say X_1, Richardson's equation for the rate of change in this nation's arms is

$$dX_1/dt = g - aX_1 + kX_2$$

where X_2 refers to the level of arms in a second nation. Similar equations may then be written for this second nation or, indeed, any number of additional nations.

Of critical importance are the labels and therefore the interpretations one gives to the three kinds of parameters. Richardson referred to the first parameter g as a "grievance" term, though he allowed for negative grievances so as to include nations having nonbellicose or pacifistic orientations. He referred to the coefficient of the nation's own level of arms, namely a, as a "fatigue" coefficient indicating the degree to which the nation concerned would tend to slow down its rate of increase in its arms production as its existing level of arms became substantial, presumably owing to the drain of arms production on other kinds of needed goods. Finally, he referred to the coefficient k of the second nation's arms level X_2 as a "defense" or "sensitivity" coefficient. Presumably, then, this simple model suggests that one look for three kinds of factors influencing a nations' rate of arms build-up.

Now suppose one wishes to generalize the theory, say to include conflicts between two (or more) ethnic groups, rival gangs, or perhaps a marital pair. The notions of grievance, fatigue, and sensitivity make good sense and, indeed, the model seems roughly appropriate. Unfortunately, however, the model is so simple that alternative formulations yield precisely the same kind of equation system. Robert Abelson (1963) begins with a radically different perspective, namely that of two parties responding to each other's prior acts, but with a memory decay or "forgiveness" parameter. The idea is that each takes into consideration not only the most recent act of the other, but an entire set of prior acts. The coefficients of such prior acts, however, become smaller and smaller as one goes back in time, so that earlier acts are discounted in accord with some lawlike decay factor that may vary from one party to another. Abelson refers to such a parameter as a "forgiveness" coefficient, arguing that some actors may in effect have much longer memories than others. He then shows that this type of formulation is identical, mathematically, to Richardson's arms race model, except that the grievance terms have been omitted.

Both Richardson and Abelson refer to "sensitivity" coefficients, but whereas Richardson explains arms race phenomena (and, presumably, other types of conflict situations) in terms of "fatigue,," Abelson's identical parameter is interpreted as "forgiveness" or in terms of memory decay. Clearly these are fundamentally different interpretations for what are mathematically the same parameters. How could this have come about? And what are the more general implications for formalization efforts in terms of relatively simple mathematical models?

The problem stems from the fact that both Richardson's and Abelson's models, although sophisticated, are both extremely simple relative to the real world complexities they are attempting to model. Why should the coefficient of X_1 be interpreted as a single kind of variable, rather than a representation of the myriad of factors that operate in basically the same way, namely as multipliers of the X_1 term? Had the coefficient a (or g or k) been treated as a *variable* that needed to be explained in its own right, then a whole series of possible causes could have been considered, one of which might be "fatigue" and another "forgiveness." Indeed, as one increases the scope of one's theory and then asks whether such "constants" would be expected to remain invariant under a wide variety of so-called scope conditions, one would undoubtedly reach a negative conclusion. But if, indeed, each "constant" in the original and simplified model also requires explanation, the theoretical formulation would have to be far more complex. In the example under consideration, both the Richardson and the Abelson formulations would have to be considered as special cases. The fact that, in the simplest of cases, they imply identical systems of differential equations does not imply that a more general formulation could not allow for *both* kinds of labels for the coefficient of X_1

Thus I see basically two kinds of drawbacks of extremely simple mathematical (or logical) formulations: (1) they may lock in prematurely on a small set of explanatory mechanisms that, when put to the test, explain only a very small proportion of the variance; and (2) they may result in overly simplistic labels (and thus interpretations) for whatever "constants" appear in the models. Of course one may refuse to give such constants any labels at all, but if so the equations remain totally abstract and therefore substantively useless. They may remain the plaything of the mathematical sociologist without having much of an impact on the larger sociological enterprise.

Another form of systematic theorizing takes off in a direction recommended by Hans Zetterberg (1965) as so-called Axiomatic Theory. Basically, this approach involves assembling a series of definitions and axioms, and then attempting to move deductively from these to a set of theorems. As noted quite some time ago by Costner and Leik (1963), however, such deductive theories run into difficulty as soon as one allows for disturbance terms in equations representing the effects of omitted variables. In the case of even a moderately long simple causal chain, for example, empirical associations between end variables are likely to become extremely small. If V causes W, which in turn affects X, which affects Y, which affects Z, if each of the "direct" associations yields a total correlation of .6, the predicted association between V and Z will be only .13, implying an explained variance of merely 1.7 percent. Such a very weak association could, of course, be accounted for by a large number of alternative mechanisms. More generally, as soon as one allows for stochastic disturbance terms under the very reasonable assumption that not even the best of theories can be all-inclusive, much of the deductive power of the theory will be destroyed.

What this implies, practically, is that patterns involving highly indirect effects or patterns of association produced by relatively remote sources of spuriousness will be exceedingly difficult to predict theoretically. Only the more immediate causal factors and sources of spuriousness can be located or inferred by empirical means. The kinds of relatively subtle theoretical arguments advanced by persons calling themselves theorists will, at best, be amenable to very weak empirical tests. Perhaps the sign of an indirect linkage can be predicted with better than chance probability, but magnitudes of relationships will seldom be predicted by deductively formulated theories. And where the linkage between two variables, say W and Z, is mediated by two or more variables, say X and Y, not even the sign of the total association will be predictable unless the linkages involving the intervening variables are in the same direction. Weak theory indeed!

As soon as one allows for multiple correlation and the likelihood that many such causal variables will, themselves, be causally interrelated, attempts to develop formal theories by listing propositions and definitions, quickly get out of hand. Most likely, the relationships *among* a phenomenon's causes will tend to be neglected, so that the basic causal models implied will tend to look like a simple fan, with supposedly unconnected variables X_1 all directly affecting Y, or perhaps doing so through only one or two other variables.

Feedback loops among variables are also likely either to be neglected or treated in a casual manner, so that they are then likely to be ignored in data analyses that assume there is a single dependent variable, rather than a *set* of mutually interdependent endogenous variables. Behaviors of school children are taken as dependent, rather than feeding back to influence those of their parents or teachers. Behaviors of delinquents do not affect those of court officials, and so forth. The real world's complexities are so simplified, at least in the propositions that investigators actually test, that misleading interpretations are almost bound to result. This, in turn, may help to stimulate needless theoretical debates that could only be resolved by more sophisticated data analyses motivated by the formulation of more inclusive theories allowing for such complexities.

Parsimony is often inadvertently achieved theoretically through the common practice of setting up theories as *alternatives* to one another, rather than as being complementary. Where schools of thought form around one or another orientation, the tendency is to argue forcefully in favor of one's own favorite set of explanatory variables or mechanisms as being somehow opposed to those of members of other schools. The result is a deliberate selection of a small subset of explanatory variables and then an effort to use this set to attempt to account for a variety of dependent variables. The empirical counterpart of such a tack is to attempt to rule out one's opponent's set of variables by showing that they explain a smaller percentage of the total variance than one's own set does, once the variables from the other set have been controlled.

Sometimes differences between the explanatory power of the "rival" sets are marginal. On other occasions, methodological artifacts can be adduced to account for whatever differences have been found. For instance, if one measures one's own variables much more carefully than one's opponent's, or if the research design virtually holds the latter constant, then the dice are being loaded in one's own favor. Furthermore, endless debates are likely to occur as to which of the theories needs to be discarded and which retained. Someone genuinely interested in obtaining a more complete set of explanatory mechanisms would, of course, start from the other end: with a set of delimited phenomena to be explained and an eclectic orientation to the selection of independent variables. Such a person would likely be impatient with those theorists who insist that only their own particular orientation is in some way "valid." Such a theorist and data analyst would have a hard time reaching a meeting of minds, with the result that the latter could easily become impatient with the former. Although I have perhaps overstated the tendencies in such instances, I believe that the relatively narrower orientation of many theorists may be one of the reasons for the present unfortunate situation in which theorists and empiricists are failing to work closely together.

In summary, I believe that many of our problems stem from a tendency to strive toward theoretical parsimony, whether because this is thought necessary in order to develop formal theories or because it is the natural resultant of the formation of supposedly rival schools of thought. We have learned to strive for parsimony from reading the philosophy of science literature, which emphasizes the principle of Occam's razor as one of the most important criteria in evaluating scientific theories. Such a principle works well in pure mathematics, where the "elegance" of a proof is conceived in terms of its simplicity, as well as the generality of the theorem in question. Theoretical physicists also strive toward parsimony in their explanatory laws.

In other sciences, parsimonious explanations may remain the ideal, but are not really expected. In sociology, as I have argued elsewhere (Blalock 1982, 1986), a strong case can be made that if one wants theories that are simultaneously general in scope but also realistic in terms of their ability to explain variance, then parsimony will probably have to be sacrificed. One illustration of this point is the above-noted problem of having to relax one's assumptions about "constants" whenever the scope of a generalization is increased. This point applies not only to one's theory but even to the "constants" that appear in empirical regression equations. But if parsimony must be foregone, the implications for theory construction are profound.

AN EXAMPLE: "ADDING UP" A COMPLEX FIELD

When I was a graduate student trying to cope with the vast literature on race relations, I came across Robin Williams' *The Reduction of Intergroup Tensions* (1947). This work contained, among other things, some one hundred theoretical propositions arranged by topic and ordered to produce a reasonably systematic flow from one proposition to the next, as well as containing explicit definitions of important concepts. I do not know whether Williams' work constituted the first such attempt by a sociologist to construct a systematic theory, but it certainly served as a model for me. Much more compatible with the parsimony strategy was George Homans' *The Human Group* (1950), which involved an important effort to build a theory around a very small number of basic concepts—sentiments, activities, interaction, norms, and the distinction between internal and external systems.

I was torn between these two strategies of theory building, but when I decided to try to make sense of the very diffuse body of literature dealing with macro-comparative race relations I encountered a major obstacle. Although there were plenty of factual materials and lengthy explanations, as well as a somewhat common vocabulary, I could find very few actual theoretical propositions. When I tried to transform authors' explanations into propositions of the sort that Williams had produced, there were such large gaps involved that nothing hung together. One proposition linked variables A and B, another variables C and D. and a third variables E and F. I also discovered that, for the most part, Williams' propositions were social psychological in nature and did not link at all well with the macro-comparative race relations literature. I was at an impasse, though I made a valiant effort in my dissertation to make it appear as though the propositions I developed hung together in a very loose sort of way.

I believe that this type of experience, if foisted on current graduate students, might be one very effective mechanism for getting across the message conveyed in Gibbs' chapter, namely that discursive theories are grossly inadequate and highly confusing to the serious reader. Those who attempt to summarize large bodies of literature for the purpose of writing textbooks undoubtedly encounter the same kind of difficulty with discursive theories. Perhaps one of the reasons we tend to group theoretical works into "schools" of thought, and then leave it at that, is that it is exceedingly difficult to transform highly diffuse arguments into succinct propositions that may then be systematically compared.

Much more recently I have had a similar experience attempting to integrate portions of the highly diffuse bodies of literature dealing with power and social conflict (Blalock 1989a). By this time, I had come to recognize that propositional formats are not sufficiently compact to handle large numbers of variables. For example, with only 20 variables, there are $20(19)/2 = 190$ separate bivariate relationships that could be specified and that, indeed, would need to be taken into consideration in a reasonably complete theory. If one had forty variables, the number of pairs would be 780, making it obviously impossible for a reader to keep track of the logic of the argument stated in propositional format, even assuming all relationships to be linear and no statistical interactions involving three or more variables. Of course one could make the wildly simplified assumption that no "independent" variables in the system are causally interrelated—or that such relationships, where they exist, can be conveniently ignored in the theory—but this is precisely the kind of simplifying assumption that I believe gets us into trouble.

In the causal models I ultimately constructed to handle the kinds of complexities I found in the verbal theories I tried to integrate, what I referred to as the general model of conflict processes contained forty variables for *each* of the parties in a conflict situation. The model was largely recursive but contained several feedback loops and a number of pairs of variables assumed to be reciprocally related. Even this model was far from complete, and so I also developed a number of submodels dealing with additional complications encountered in specific kinds of conflict situations. One of these, involving twenty-seven variables, dealt with added complications produced by a party's heterogeneity and problems encountered in the mobilization process. Another involved a set of ideological dimensions needed to explain macro-level conflicts and contained a set of twenty-seven variables, only some of which overlapped those involved in the previous models. Finally, it required a gigantic causal model containing fifty-six variables (for each party) to deal with the processes of sustaining and terminating conflicts already underway. Had these fifty-six variables been linked by means of a complete set of bivariate propositions—many of which would have implied no direct causal linkages, or no relationships with other variables controlled—the total number of propositions would have come to 1,540.

Many readers will doubtlessly conclude that it is ridiculous to introduce such a large number of variables into a theoretical system. Yet my own reading of the literature is that even a modestly complete theory of conflict processes, if faithful to the discursive literature, must contain such variables, at least as a starting point. Then, as the theory is applied to specific cases, simplifying assumptions can be made. Some variables will be effectively held constant in the setting or period being examined. Some forms of conflict, as for example those involving a marital dyad, can simply bypass a number of the variables needed to account for mobilization efforts by loosely knit quasi-groups such as racial or ethnic minorities. And other conflicts may be of short enough duration that changes in utilities and beliefs can be ignored. But one always does so at the risk of making unjustified simplifications that are often swept under the rug and therefore hidden from view. Such assumptions, although possibly reasonable in the case of a particular kind of conflict, may be highly problematic in the case of others. Whenever one attempts to construct a general theory covering a reasonably large number of different kinds of conflict, the number of variables, and therefore the complexity of the model, will almost certainly increase very substantially.

WHY THE LACK OF INTEREST AND WHAT CAN BE DONE?

In addition to the very important theoretical and methodological obstacles to developing systematic theories that are both realistic and testable, I believe there are several important disciplinary shortcomings that are also largely responsible for the present rather unsatisfactory state of affairs. First, sociology does not attract the quality of students needed to support the enterprise. In particular, the overwhelming majority of sociologists are *neither* theoretically nor methodologically inclined or sophisticated. Second, both our undergraduate and graduate training programs are highly inadequate, in the sense of providing the necessary socialization to motivate and train members of the discipline to appreciate and take advantage of what few systematic theories we do have available, nor are they socialized to be dissatisfied with the status quo. Mundane empirical research and superficial interpretive accounts have become the norm within our discipline. Finally, our publication policies and lack of organization to undertake coordinated research efforts aimed at genuine cumulation of knowledge, encourage more of the same. The result is

a series of small-scale, individualistic research projects scattered among
n extremely large and growing domain of unconnected substantive topics
involving very low levels of abstraction and time- and space-bound empirical findings.

Many indicators suggest that sociology attracts students having low SAT
and GRE scores, very poor mathematics and science backgrounds, little or
no interest in the philosophy of science, and only a very superficial knowledge of sociological theory. Even our brighter graduate students frequently
become seduced, as research assistants, into focusing almost entirely on relatively narrow research topics, often as members of a team supported by a
large-scale research grant obtained by one or more faculty members. They
almost immediately become immersed in the details of the project itself, taking theory and methods courses on the side along with a series of relatively
disjointed substantive seminars. Rarely are they forced to link the latter
courses with what they have learned in theory courses, nor are the latter specifically enough focused to facilitate any kind of synthesizing or generalizing
process. The result is a compartmentalized training program in which *both*
theory and methods courses are merely incidental to the student's practicum
research experience. Worse still, if students move from one project to another
their vitae and interests look very much like scattershot: a little bit of this, a
little bit of that, and perhaps enough training in several substantive areas that
they are in a position to teach a variety of courses at the undergraduate level.

Thus students lack both the inclination and prior training needed to pursue any theoretical topic in depth. When they search for "relevant" theory
they may indeed come up with a list of theoretical propositions suited for
rough translation into testable research hypotheses, but the *logical* (or mathematical) structure in the underlying theoretical arguments is of little concern
to them. In effect, they are taught to apply an empirical approach to theoretical arguments, namely to conduct a literature review so as to come up with
an eclectic set of researchable questions. In Mertons' (1949) terms, they may
be concerned with "empirical generalizations," but not their logical or
causal interconnections. When causal diagrams are presented and when path
coefficients are attached to these diagrams, for example, these are rarely ac-
companied by any kind of thorough discussion of the underlying theory, the
latent or theoretical variables that have been omitted or only imperfectly measured, or concerns about generalizability or problems of measurement com-
parability. In short, causal models are treated in the same perfunctory manner
as are serious efforts to construct verbal theories. It would perhaps be an ex-
aggeration to suggest that the theoretical portions of the resulting papers are
mere window dressing, but given journal-editors' propensities to encourage
brevity, the theoretical side of most such papers is often extremely weak.

Graduate students who are socialized to "produce" publications by serving as junior authors of faculty-sponsored research projects often serve more in the role of data-analysis specialists than theorists, a practice that merely reinforces the notion that "someone else" should have the responsibility of producing the theory. Clearly, a division of labor is both necessary and almost inevitable in any discipline, but if the preponderance of graduate training leaves the theoretical side to more senior personnel, how is the student to make the transition?

One need not be entirely pessimistic in this regard, provided that we make a very conscious effort to develop mechanisms within our graduate training programs to supplement the more mundane aspects of research training with serious "thought" projects involving tough intellectual challenges. These could include theory construction projects, papers involving careful conceptualization efforts, searches for ways to introduce approaches from other disciplines into sociology, attempts to cross-cut several substantive areas by formulating problems and questions at a higher level of generalizability, and searches for significant data gaps and unresolved but important questions in one's field (Blalock forthcoming).

During the 1960s especially, sociology departments succumbed to pressures to reduce the number of required courses to an absolute minimum. Even in those departments that require, say, a year of statistics, we must begin virtually from scratch and assume no knowledge even of elementary calculus. In my own department, we offer a number of more advanced and technical seminars in quantitative methods, but only a handful of students take more than the minimum required. Really demanding theory courses are also a thing of the past if, indeed, they ever existed. One or two required survey courses, usually involving a study of the writings of dead sociologists, are often all that is required. Perhaps there are a handful of sociology departments that require students to construct their own theories, but it is my distinct impression that for the most part graduate students are exposed much more to the so-called classics than to more recent efforts to develop systematic theories. Rarely, if at all, is either type of experience closely linked with the students' training in empirical research or even a close reading of the more theoretical literature within whatever substantive fields they have selected as areas of concentration. In short, our training programs are both compartmentalized and generally lacking in real depth. They represent little more than slightly advanced undergraduate programs.

Students rather naturally pattern their behaviors after those of their mentors. They read journal articles based primarily on secondary data analyses in which investigators take data gaps and poor measurement more or less for granted, selecting as measures of dependent variables whatever indicators happen to be available. Their lists of independent variables contain, perhaps, a few attitude scales, a number of superficial "background" variables (e.g., race, sex, age, or father's occupation), and perhaps a few contextual factors or setting variables. Most such indicators, of course, connect only very poorly with conceptually defined variables of interest to theorists, and so the above-noted tendency to select a few rough indicators becomes common practice. Serious follow-up studies involving much more carefully measured variables, more inclusive sets of independent variables, and specifications of temporal or dynamic models are indeed rare. The student learns that it seldom pays to dig in and study a single topic over a prolonged period of time, especially when other secondary data are readily available.

Much of the problem, then, stems from the way we are organized—or not organized—to collect and analyse data. Ideally, there should be considerable exploratory research, careful conceptualization and reconceptualization of one's theoretical problem based on the preliminary analysis of such exploratory investigations, and finally a much more serious collective effort made to conduct more ambitious studies involving large numbers of variables and carefully formulated theories specifying predicted relationships among such variables. Such an effort would not only be very time consuming and expensive, but it would require considerably more scholarly collaboration than we are presently organized to produce. Definitive publications would have to be delayed long beyond the time periods needed to make tenure decisions, and junior scholars would probably have to take a back seat to their more senior mentors. Even more difficult, perhaps, would be the active collaboration of persons who refer to themselves as "theorists" with those who are primarily data analysts.

The products of such really serious efforts would also be difficult for most sociologists to digest, and there would be an overwhelming temptation, especially in the book literature, to water down the materials to a kind of least common denominator among potential readers. This would typically involve omitting the subtleties, including discussions of untested assumptions and the operation of possible omitted variables, careful theoretical definitions and distinctions, and technical methodological complications. It would also probably involve drastic oversimplifications of theoretical arguments and considerations of generalizability and how scope conditions could be modified if the book were also addressed to a lay or popular audience, publishers would undoubtedly also insist that the presentation be as painless as possible for untrained readers. Another more or less typical empirical sociological work would be the result. Technical details and other subtleties would be reserved for specialized journals.

Finally, I am deeply concerned about the overwhelming thrust toward applied sociology. Applications of any discipline are, of course, both welcomed and of considerable motivating interest to most of us. The normative climate within our discipline, however, has developed in the direction of encouraging almost anything, just so long as a "sociological perspective" is used. Since such a term is, at best, extremely vague, we are giving ourselves a hunting licence to study any topic "of interest" to anyone who calls him/herself a sociologist. Subfields are proliferating at a dizzying pace, and with this has come a lowering of levels of abstraction. This, in itself, would not constitute a serious intellectual problem if we had a series of reasonably general theories for which such a wide variety of applications could be shown to be special cases. But we do not, and so the "theories" used are merely window dressing.

Add to this the fact that we tend to invoke the same old explanatory factors and background variables, and our analyses give outsiders the impression of being entirely too superficial. Sometimes we are good journalists and call the general public's attention to previously unrecognized social problems. For instance, sociologists were among the first to highlight the extent to which domestic violence and child abuse have become endemic in our society. The basic question, however, is whether we have the theoretical and methodological tools to push our analyses of such problems beyond the commonsense level. Without systematically oriented theory, I do not believe we can do so.

CONCLUDING REMARKS

There is very little we can do, at least in the near future, about some of the problems I have discussed. To increase the quality of our undergraduate majors and graduate applicants will require a sustained effort which, thus far, has not materialized. I am also not optimistic about the improvement of the mathematics backgrounds of the typical graduate student, though we may perhaps be able to coordinate our activities so as to provide special training opportunities, perhaps at the postdoctoral level, for the select few who can be enticed along this path. Perhaps several four to eight week theory-construction and/or math-modeling workshops could once more become a reality, although such programs were tried without too much success during the 1950s and 1960s.

Nor am I very optimistic about our chances of impacting on journal-editing practices, to say nothing of the even more diverse book literature and commercially inclined editors. A monograph series, however, might be much more feasible, and I believe we should take a serious look at this kind of publication outlet. Perhaps a portion of the Arnold Rose Monograph Series could be allocated to this type of enterprise, with a special editor appointed by the ASA.

I do believe that relatively modest efforts to modify our graduate training programs could be sold to our colleagues, as long as we do not attempt to make drastic alterations that would greatly prolong the period of graduate study. Above all else, there needs to be a much more active coordination and communication process between those who teach theory courses and those of us who emphasize the kind of methodological training that places the emphasis more on theoretical understanding of basic methodological issues than on the mastery of the latest statistical technique or packaged program. Bringing theory and research together has been a worthy goal for quite some time, but we have given only token attention to the task. Without an explicit and organized effort to move the profession in this direction, I am not at all optimistic that favorable changes will be forthcoming.

The basic practical problem we face is that of convincing our colleagues that such changes are really needed. The more "case studies" we have of careful theoretical work that has actually been useful in guiding research agendas, the easier it should be to make a convincing argument.

8

Formal Theory Construction in Gender Sociology: An Unexploited Gold Mine of Possibilities

Janet Saltzman Chafetz

I can count on one hand the sociologists I know who make any explicit attempt at formal theory construction in the area of gender/feminist sociology. Several hands would be required to count the number of feminist scholars who explicitly reject formal theory on the basis that it is antithetical to a "feminist consciousness." Add a number of feet to those hands and one could count the gender/feminist theorists who write theory in discursive style, regardless of whether they explicitly reject the appropriateness of formal theory. Without claiming that my work is a sophisticated example of formal theory, since I count myself among those who make the attempt (e.g., Chafetz 1984, 1990; Chafetz and Dworkin 1986), I obviously think that the effort is both desireable and feasible.

In this chapter I will first attempt to explain the erroneous logic that leads many feminist sociologists to reject the enterprise of formal theory construction as irrelevant, biased, and indeed harmful to women's interests. In the second section I will address some of the fundamental problems that confront those theorists who do not automatically reject the effort, by arguing that gender sociology shares three problems with the discipline more generally that impede the development of formal theory. Finally, I will demonstrate that there is much about gender sociology that makes the application of formal theory construction especially feasible and promising.

A FEMINIST CASE AGAINST FORMAL THEORY

Feminist scholars rarely explicitly argue against formal theory construction per se. Rather, many reject the possibility of a "positivist" sociology that

137

searches for panhistorical and cross-cultural generalizations applicable to the behavior of human individuals and aggregates. They argue as well against deductive theory. I take this to automatically imply the rejection of any attempt to: (1) state theory in propositional (not to mention mathmatical) form; (2) focus on logical relationships among constructs and among propositions; and (3) specify *a priori* the methods by which a theory can be tested and potentially falsified. In turn, I see these as the central elements of formal theory construction that differentiate it from discursive techniques for the presentation of theoretical ideas.

Contemporary gender sociologists—including myself—are almost without exception primarily motivated to specialize in gender because of our ideological/political commitment to feminism. Although there are many definitions of "feminism," a core political commitment unites all who label themselves as feminists, namely, a commitment to battle that which they perceive as disadvantaging or devaluing women on the basis of their gender. Further, feminists agree that in virtually all contemporary societies there exist social practices which serve to disadvantage/devalue women. Gender specialists who are feminist agree, at least implicitly, that the sociological study of gender should devote itself substantially to describing those disadvantages and their effects, analyzing how they arise, and especially how they are maintained and might be changed. Because of this political motivation, gender theory is at least implicitly—and often outspokenly—oriented to issues of public policy.

Feminist sociologists share a consensus on one more, major issue: the androcentric bias of traditional (and some contemporary) sociology that arises from the fact that, until the 1970s, almost all sociologists were (white) men. It is some of the ramificiations of that bias that are open to considerable dispute. Undisputed are the following:

1. Women were largely ignored by traditional sociology outside of the study of the family and some aspects of demography, specifically fertility. For instance, the study of work was primarily of men's labor participation force; of stratification and social mobility of men as family heads; of juvenile delinquency of mostly male adolescent gangs.

2. Topics centrally important to the lives of many women were largely ignored by traditional sociology: for instance, the study of unpaid *work* in the household and volunteer realms; the sociology of emotions; conflict, power, and the unequal distribution of resources *within* the family or household.

3. The experiences, values, behaviors, and priorities of men were implicitly taken as the norm against which women were compared—and usually found wanting. Related to this, research done on exclusively male samples

was simply assumed, often erroneously, to generalize to women, such as the relationship between educational and income attainment.

In short, the historical exclusion of women from sociology resulted in the exclusion of women as research subjects, in ignoring a variety of topics, and in bias in interpreting women's experiences. In turn, these biases functioned to support and legitimate a social system that has been inequitable to women.

But some feminist sociologists have gone well beyond these topical and interpretive biases to insist that the basic *methodology and epistemology* of traditional sociology are masculine, biased, and hence antithetical to a feminist consciousness (e.g., Smith 1979, 1987, 1989; Farganis 1986). The *implicit* reasoning is what I interpret to be an erroneous syllogism:

a) Men created sociology, including the epistemological foundations and methodological techniques of the field.

b) Sociological knowledge was traditionally biased against women and harmful to women's interests.

c) *Therefore*, the traditional epistemology and methods of sociology are inherently biased against women and harmful to their interests.

In short, methodology and epistemology, their application, and the results of that application are intertwined and confused. I certainly agree that the techniques of traditional theory development and research in sociology have often been misapplied, resulting in bias. The questions are: (1) is such misapplication inherent in the techniques and therefore uncorrectable? and (2) what alternatives exist that improve the situation?

More specifically, those scholars who call themselves "feminist theorists/epistemologists" argue that traditional approaches, which presumably include formal theory construction, treat research subjects as "objects" of the external world to be "manipulated" by researchers who fail to respect their humanity. In this way, sociology becomes an instrument of control rather than of "liberation" (Smith 1987, 1989; Farganis 1986). "Doing" feminist sociology is said to require "praxis" (Cook and Fonow 1986; Miles 1983; Westcott 1979). The feminist sociologist does not set herself apart from, or as superior to the subjects of her research. Rather, she supports the subjects in what is presumed to be the subjects' search for liberation from "oppressive"—especially "patriarchal"—social conditions. The researcher's agenda is supposedly set by the subjects' agenda (which, in fact, may be antithetical to feminists' agenda in many instances, a conflict rarely recognized or discussed by these sociologists). Therefore, the "appropriate" research method is intensive, case study or small sample interviews concerning the everyday world of subjects, with a premium placed on subjects' interpretation of that world. The appropriate theory is inductive and interpretive, and eschews substantial generalization or abstraction (e.g., 1974; Kasper 1986). From this perspective, deductive theory, large-scale quantitative research, and macro-structural analyses are "masculine" and fundamentally antithetical to feminism.

Virtually the same critique has been heard for over twenty years from many men who scarcely consider themselves feminist theorists or gender sociologists. In light of this, it has long puzzled me why those feminist scholars who accepted this approach have labeled it specifically feminist. What puzzles me even more is the fact that at least some feminists who argue in the manner I just discussed have violated their own logic when it comes to specific theories. While "positivism," and presumably formal theory construction are unusable because they are "masculine," the misogynistic theory of Freud has received considerable attention by feminists devoted to maintaining its central insights while stripping it of its masculine biases (the same is true also of Marxian but not Parsonian theory). There is an interesting sociology of knowledge question lurking beneath these choices of what to revamp and what to simply dismiss.

Underlying the rejection of what they define as a "masculine epistemology" is a highly questionable assumption about how women and men think, which is itself substantially rooted in feminist neo-Freudian theory. As described and critiqued especially well by Epstein (1988), many contemporary feminists have come to accept the quite old (and often antifemininst) argument that men and women think in qualitatively different ways. Women are said to be more relational and contextual in their cognitive processes, and less willing to or interested in divorcing emotion from cognition. Men are said to be more analytical, separative, and inclined to divorce feelings from cognitions (see, for instance, Stacey and Thorne 1985). Ergo, so this reasoning goes, men and women in sociology, especially feminist women who have avoided "masculinist brainwashing," use different epistemologies in their work (with the implication that the women's approach is "better"). These differences, in turn, are usually said to be rooted in infant and early childhood experiences, as argued by feminist neo-Freudian theorists such as Nancy Chodorow (1979), or sometimes in women's maternal experiences and familial roles.

I have seen no convincing empirical evidence to demonstrate such gender differences in cognitive processes among adult women and men engaged in similar work, nor have I seen empirical evidence that demonstrates a substantial linkage between childhood, gender-related experiences and adult cognitive processes, net of other variables. Along with Epstein (1988) and Coser (1989), I reject the notion that male and female sociologists think in ways that are fundamentally different from one another, which is not to deny that they may often differ in what topics they think about. I firmly believe that formal theory construction, quantitative analyses and so on, can be, and are presently used in the interests of women, that is, divorced from their traditional androcentric biases. Further, I think that a lot of male ethnomethodologists, critical, postmodern, existential, and symbolic interactionist theorists might question whether the reason for their chosen approaches is that they think like women! Finally, what self-styled feminist epistemologists propose seems to me to be a sociology composed of two things: endless ''contextual'' description of unique phenomena at the micro level, and untestable, unfalsifiable ''metatheory.'' The latter returns us to eighteenth-century armchair speculation. The former is no different from the mindless empiricism everyone says they bemoan, even though numbers aren't crunched. Ironically given the feminist commitment to change, neither has substantial power to inform public policy debates or sway policy-makers.

PROBLEMS CONFRONTING FORMAL THEORY CONSTRUCTION IN GENDER SOCIOLOGY

I believe that there are three central problems that make formal theory construction in gender sociology rare, even among those who do not reject it epistemologically. These problems are in no way unique to this particular specialty, however. They are: (1) the absence of people trained to think rigorously in theoretical terms; (2) the absence of clear, central theoretical questions; (3) the poverty of our central concepts, specifically their definitions.

Theory Training

Formal theory is substantive theory; it is an explanation of some empirically observable, and presumably measurable phenomenon. ''Theory'' taught in theory courses and seminars is largely metatheory written discursively, and often so abstractly as to refer specifically to nothing that one can directly observe. Substantive theory is generally taught as part of substantive courses. ''Theory specialists'' in sociology do talmudic exegesis of great dead folk and incomprehensible live European thinkers (which is also much of what is taught in theory classes), and esoteric analyses of metatheoretical and epistemological issues. In short, self-denied theorists in sociology rarely explain concrete, empirical phenomena, and people who do so rarely define themselves as theory specialists. The result is that ''theory'' in sociology is a set of diverse answers to esoteric questions most other sociologists rarely ask or care about.

Until ''theory'' ceases to be an esoteric specialty area and becomes part-and-parcel of the everyday sociological enterprise, we cannot hope to develop any sizeable number of sociologists capable of and interested in constructing formal theory in any area. Even when formal theory construction is taught, my hunch is that it is taught in the abstract and largely divorced from the everyday doing of sociology. So, generations of neophyte sociologists learn how to tack some "theory" on the front end of their research reports and "derive" some testable hypotheses from that discussion, thereby legitimating their work as "theoretically relevant."

The teachers of theory must totally revamp their courses to teach how discursive substantive theory, and even some metatheory, can be rendered into formal theory about some empirical issue. I call this approach teaching "theory in use." The content of such a course is one or a few different substantive areas, and the diverse contemprary theories and theoretical perspectives actually used or applied in those areas. The goal is to examine what a variety of theoretical approaches say or imply about a central, substantive question, and how they can be combined and used to generate potentially *testable* explanations of that phenomenon.

For instance, in gender sociology we have a large variety of contemporary theoretical approaches that, at least implicitly, attempt to explain how systems of gender stratification maintain and reproduce themselves. These approaches reflect such diverse traditions as Marxian, Freudian, symbolic interaction, labeling, exchange, Weberian, social role, social learning, and ethnomethodological "theory" (see Chafetz 1988). By examining different contemporary perspectives on *one question*, students can be moved toward seeing that they are not mutually exclusive or contradictory, that they can be substantially integrated, and that they can be rendered into a formally stated, potentially testable theory that attempts to explain gender system stability.

In short, I propose that for sociologists to create formal theory they must learn how to do it. To learn how to do it, as students they must be walked through exercises in formal theory construction in one or more concrete cases, using contemporary theory about empirically substantive issues. Surely, a discipline that routinely trains graduate students in the application of highly sophisticated statistical techniques to their sociological research can do as well in terms of formal theory instruction.

Posing Theoretical Questions

Sociology in general, gender sociology no more nor less than the rest of the field, is a grab bag of "answers" going in search of important and coherent theoretical questions. "Theory" addresses issues that range on a continuum from so abstract that they are untestable, to highly concrete, time- or place-specific phenomena that aren't really theoretical. In gender sociology, what passes for theory addresses such diverse questions as: how are children engendered? what explains male violence against women? what explains gender labor force segregation? the persistent gap between men's and women's wages? cross-cultural variation in the level of gender stratification? how is gender inequality reproduced in everyday, interpersonal interactions? why do women do most of the childrearing and domestic work? what explains the rise and growth of women's movements? why was ERA defeated and why are some women antifeminist? how do race, class and gender intersect? what explains wives' relative power of autonomy within the family? how do "patriarchy" and capitalism affect and support one another? The list could go on considerably longer.

Questions are posed on the basis of practical or political concerns, specific metatheoretical attachments (e.g., to Marxian, Freudian, symbolic interaction, or some other metatheory), or any of a number of idiosyncratic bases. The answers do not add up to a *coherent* explanation of any major theoretical question. Nor do answers tend to cumulate, leading to theoretical development and refinement. Indeed, such "theories" are usually *applied* to data—often ex post facto—rather than *tested* empirically. This practice almost always and automatically produces "support" for theory; falsification and refinement require systematic theory testing. I interpret the purpose of formal theory construction as precisely the ongoing, cumulative development and refinement of explanation through systematic testing. While one can formulate important theoretical questions and fail to address them formally, formal theory construction worth constructing must begin with coherent, theoretically meaningful questions. I suggest that our discipline, and my specialty, have mostly failed to come to any consensus concerning the basic theoretical questions that require answers. This step is preliminary to formal theory construction, for the latter is hardly worth the effort in the absence of the former.

Conceptual Poverty

The basic building blocks of theory are theoretical constructs. Formal theory requires not only that the central terms be clearly defined conceptually, but also that most be readily amenable to operationalization. Most, if not all terms should refer to phenomena that vary, that is, they should be defined so as to enable the use of a quantitative logic when linking terms in propositions. Sociology, including gender sociology, abounds in constructs/concepts that are defined so that they are truth-asserting, difficult or impossible to agree upon appropriate empirical indicators, used in a reified manner, and altogether vague (see Gibbs 1989 for a highly astute discussion of the problems with sociological constructs and their definitions). In addition, many are not readily usable with a quantitative logic. In gender sociology, among the most commonly used theoretical terms are "patriachy," "sexism," "gender role," and "the oppression of women." They all share the problems enumerated above, and therefore pose major obstacles to the development of formal theory—or even good theory that is not stated formally. For the sake of brevity, I will examine only one of thsese terms: patriarchy. This discussion, however, is equally applicable to the others.

Various feminist theorists use the term "patriarchy" to refer to ideology (secular and/or religious), to properties of the family, economy or polity, or to some combination thereof. Because the term has entered the popular feminist idiom, it has been rendered even more broad and vague than might otherwise have been the case. Clearly, it is heavily laden with ideological and pejorative meaning. To the extent that it refers to more than one of the several institutions listed above, it is truth-asserting. Questions concerning the nature of, and processes that connect gender inequity in these various realms cannot be raised or answered because they are simply assumed to be empirically isomorphic. "Patriarchy" refers to an abstract property distilled from human behaviors and utterances. It is therefore reification to use any active verb with it. Yet throughout the gender literature one finds patriarchy "requiring," "producing," "creating," "causing," "needing," "encouraging," and so on. In this way, it sounds like a profound explanation is being offered when in fact nothing concrete is being uttered. One virtually never finds the term used with a quantitative logic—higher (greater) or lower (lesser) degrees or amounts of patriarchy. Yet clearly it refers in some fashion to gender inequality and we know from numerous studies that the level of gender inequality varies cross-culturally and historically on a *continuum* from very substantial female disadvantage to near equality. Given these problems, clearly one would expect to find no consensnus on how, specifically, one might adequately operationalize the term in advance of collecting data.

I have argued to this point that formal theory construction in gender sociology is seriously impeded by four things. The first is the outright rejection by some feminist scholars of the desirability of such an endeavor, a problem somewhat unique to this substantive specialty. The other three problems gender sociologists share with the discipline generally: (1) the lack of rigorous training conducive to imparting the skills required for, and the intellectual commitment to constructing formal theory; (2) the lack of a coherent agenda of theoretical questions; and (3) pervasive conceptual and definitional sloppiness. If these problems could be solved, the field of gender sociolgy is an exceptionally promising one for the development of formal theory. I will devote my remaining comments to why this specialty is unusually full of (untapped) promise in this regard.

THE PROMISE OF FORMAL THEORY CONSTRUCTION FOR GENDER SOCIOLOGY

There is no aspect of instiional life, interpersonal interaction, individual behavior, cognition, or emotion that is not in some fashion affected by gender in virtually all societies. Nor is there any aspect of social life that has no effect on gender. As a result, there is no substantive specialty in sociology where gender is irrelevant or can/should be ignored. As feminists have invaded sociology during the last two decades, consideration of gender has come to permeate almost all aspects of our discipline, and in the process an enormous quantity of research findings concerning gender has become available. This gold mine of findings gives gender theorists substantial raw material out of which to fashion theory, including formally constructed theory.

Sociologists in the United States, including those who specialize in gender, tend to be heavily ethno- and temporocentric in their research. My impression is that more cross-national and historical research is being conducted in recent years than was the case twenty years ago, but still concerns the United States today (or in the recent past). I believe that the intention of formal theory construction is to develop general explanations that refer to panhistorical and cross-cultural regularities. We do not simply seek to explain why contemporary Americans and their institutions and organizations behave, believe, or vary among themselves in some way or another. We want to answer questions that explain variations in the behaviors of *people* and *human aggregates.* To develop and test theories that are not confined to the here and now, cross-cultural and historical data are required (see Chafetz 1989).

Despite the fact that most gender sociologists do their research on contemporary residents of the United States, gender theorists have at their disposal an incredible array of data on other times and places. More so than many substantive specialties within sociology, gender specialists tend to be quite well-read in other disciplines. This has been primarily the result of the widespread development of interdisciplinary women's studies programs throughout the nation, and of a considerable number of interdisciplinary women's studies journals. In addition, given their political commitment as feminists, most gender sociologists are inclined to read the work of other feminists outside of sociology. Just as sociology has experienced an explosion of reasearch on women since the early 1970s, so too have anthropology, history, literature, psychology, linguistics, and other areas. Also, many other nations that experienced feminist movements since 1970 have enjoyed a similar explosion of knowledge about women and gender. Gender theorists can therefore call upon a rich array of data generated by other disciplines, as well as by scholars in other nations (see Chafetz 1989). This, in turn, provides rich opportunities for the development of formal theory. In my own work, I developed a theory to explain variation in the level of gender stratification (Chafetz 1984), substantially on the basis of data and insights provided by feminist anthropologists. My colleague, A. Gary Dworkin, and I developed and partially tested a theory that accounts for the emergence and growth of women's movements relying heavily on the work of feminist historians (Chafetz and Dworkin 1986).

My remaining comments focus on three ways by which gender sociology could develop formal theory in the coming years, assuming that the problems ennumerated in the earlier sections of this chapter were solved. First, I will address the development of macro-level theory. Second, I will talk about the micro level. Finally, I will briefly address a recent fad among sociological theorists: the macro-micro linkage. The distinction between the "macro" and "micro" levels has been defined in a variety of ways. For the purposes of this paper, I will use the term *macro-level* to mean research and theory that pertain to properties of aggregates, (e.g., nations, organizations, communities, states). *Macro-level* and *structural* are used synonymously. Many structural variables are no more than an aggregate of individual characteristics (e.g., the sex ratio, or the ratio of women's to men's wages in a given unit), while others represent emergent properties (e.g., feminists social movements). Regardless of variable type, macro-level analyses relate properties of collectivities to one another. My use of the term *micro-level* will therefore be confined to theory and research that focus on individual persons as the unit of analysis; that examine either attributes and behaviors of discrete persons or the behaviors of interaction partners in face-to-face settings.

Macro Gender Theory

Underlying virtually all contemporary sociological research and theory concerning gender is at least the implicit, and usually the explicit recognition of gender inequality (stratification). Even empirical and theoretical work concerning gender differentiation and the gender division of labor, which do not *logically* imply inequality, are now (unlike the days of Parsons) conducted on the premise that gender "difference" is empirically closely associated with "unequal" rewards, opportunities, and evaluations. Gender stratification (that is, the unequal access of males and females to the scarce and valued resources of their society on the basis of gender) is a fundamentally macro-level variable. Existing theories that attempt to explain its variation look to a variety of other macro-level variables, including predominant family structure, dominant ideology (especially religious but also secular), the gender division of labor both in the household and in the economy, sex ratio, technological/subsistence base of the economy, political organization, and level of economic development. While measurement problems abound in adequately operationalizing many of these constructs, at least some indicators for each are available cross-culturally. In fact, considerable comparative research has been conducted by sociologists, and especially by anthropologists, on the relationships between these variables. The anthropologists have made substantial use of the Human Area Relations Files, while the sociologists usually use government-generated data such as censuses.

There are only about a half dozen theorists who have attempted to develop macro-level gender theory in sociology that is stated formally (e.g.,

Blumberg 1984; Chafetz 1984, 1990; Chafetz and Dworkin 1986; Huber 1988; Collins 1988). The data certainly exist, generated by anthropologists and historians in addition to sociologists, to provide the necessary insights upon which to develop much more such theory. Not only are there cross-national and historical data to call upon, there exist also an abundance of state-level and metropolitan standard areas or MSA data. Moreover, there are a large number of credible theoretical ideas "floating around" in discursive theories, available to inform such efforts. Existing data and theory provide a gold mine of opportunity to sociologists who are able to and interested in constructing macro-level formal gender theory.

Micro Theory

The vast bulk of gender sociology—theoretical and empirical—pertains to individual behavior and to processes and outcomes of direct interpersonal interaction, as these affect and are affected by gender. This work is substantially ethno- and temporocentric.

While a gender stratification approach focuses largely on women and men as undifferentiated aggregates, it is clear that these categoreis are maximally heterogeneous even within one time and place. Within-gender variability on virtually any dimension is almost always substantially greater than the average differences between genders, especially in a large and complex society such as the contemporary United States (Epstein 1988). This fact provides for two general types of micro-level questions: (1) what explains variations, on the average, in the behaviors, choices, priorities, cognitive and emotional processes, and so on, of women compared to men? (2) how do we explain variation among women (or men) along those same dimensions?

The first of these questions has received the lion's share of theoretical attention in the gender litearture. Feminist neo-Freudian and socialization theories informed primarily by the symbolic interaction, social learning, and cognitive development approaches, have focused on between-gender variations of all sorts. Together, they comprise a major component of explanations of how systems of gender inequality reproduce themselves, and their ideas find their way into an astounding array of other gender theories, including even those dealing primarily with macro-level issues. Together they have also substantially exaggerated both the extent of gender difference and the importance of childhood-engendered, presumably stable "traits" of personality for understanding adult behavior (see Epstein 1988 for a review and critique of this literature). The result is rampant stereotyping of both genders. None of this has been stated as formal theory. I think that in the absence of empirical data that demonstrate both strong, consistent and stable gender-differentiated traits, and a substantially meaningful linkage between childhood engenderment and adult behaviors, this line of theorizing is now approaching a dead-end.

There is, however, another micro-level approach that shows substantially more promise. Implied by Kanter's work on men and women in the corporate world (1977; see also Miller et al. 1983), and explicitly called for recently by Risman (1987; see also Risman and Schwartz 1989), is a *micro-structural* approach to understanding differences among adult men and women. This approach looks to features of the interaction situation in an attempt to understand why men and women may behave differently from one another. Gender differences in resources, opportunities, prestige, power, general normative expectations, and social definitions, generated structurally (i.e., at the macro level) and brought to interpersonal interactions from "outside," constitute the key determinants of men's and women's behaviors in concrete interaction situations. The only formally stated version of this kind of approach I know of is provided by Blumberg's work on the effects of economic power, discounted by variable levels of ideological, political, and coercive power by men, on wives' relative marital power and autonomy (1988).

Exchange theory, with its inherent problems of tautology, is at least implicit in much micro-structural analysis. Nonetheless, I think that some key theoretical issues for gender sociology are very amenable to formalized theory (and systematic testing) from a micro-structural perspective, including: the level of deference exhibited by women to men; the level of autonomy and of power experienced by women in their marriages; and the division of household and familial labor among men and women. These basic issues, in turn, form fundamental components of broader theories of gender stratification. In order to develop micro-structural theory, the structural properties brought to interactions from "outside" (income and educational inequities, gender-specific legal or normative restrictions and obligations, etc.) will need to be rigorously defined *a priori,* and the processes by which they affect the behaviors in question will have to be more thoroughly and precisely delineated than currently is the case. Curtis' (1986) paper on social exchange within the family, while not stated in formal terms, is a step in both of these directions.

Because of an overemphasis on differences between women and men, which has resulted in a tendency to stereotype both genders, theoretical explanations of differences among women are relatively scarce. In recent years enormous attention has been paid to class and racial differences among especially American women, as exemplified by numerous conferences, meeting sessions, and special journal issues. So far, the issue has been stated as "explaining the intersection of class, race, and gender," which does not constitute a clear, *theoretically* formulated question. And, indeed, the work on this topic has been primarily descriptive. Lurking within this issue are one or more theoretical questions awaiting attention.

Virtually all of the other work on variability among women (and to a lesser extent men) has been informed by a childhood engenderment approach.

Why are some women (or girls) more oriented to gender nontraditional work than others? Because their mothers were employed outside the home or their parents were "nontraditional" in some other way. While this kind of analysis has much superficial empirical support, I do not see it going anywhere theoretically. Again, the linkage between childhood engenderment and adult behavior, *net of other variables,* has not been demonstrated empirically. In addition, its nature has not been adequately theorized beyond the questionable assumption that adult behavior represents the rather direct expression of personal traits developed early in life.

The vast amount of empirical literature at the micro level, coupled with a developing micro-structural theoretical approach, hold much promise for the development of micro-level formal theory in gender sociology. The questions amenable to such theorizing concern behavioral differences between men and women, and within each gender, in cross-gender interpersonal interactions. The answers concern the resources and expectations, generated structurally and distributed unequally by gender (as well as by class and race), that interactants bring to situations, and the processes by which these resources generate various behaviors. This area is ripe for the development of formal theory.

The Micro-Macro Linkage

The faddish issue for theory specialists in the late 1980s was how to link macro and micro theories. It has almost always been discussed in the abstract. Personally, I believe that we will get further on this and other issues of this ilk by dealing with substantive issues; that we will learn how to link the micro and macro as we wrestle with developing answers to concrete questions. Gender sociology is a particularly good field in which to address this issue, and to develop formal theory linking the various levels of analysis.

As mentioned earlier, gender permeates all levels of institutional, personal and interpersonal life, and gender theories reflect traditions that deal with all of these levels, from Marxian, indeed world systems analysis, to neo-Freudian. Virtually all gender theories recognize the importance of whichever level of analysis they short-shrift. In brief, we have the raw material out of which to fashion integrated theories that span or connect the various levels (which is what I attempted in my recent theory of stability and change in gender systems, Chafetz 1990).

In very broad terms, I see micro processes as the transmission mechanisms that connect structural independent and dependent constructs. Structural elements affect individual attitudes, cognitions, social and personal definitions, choices, and behaviors, as well as interaction behaviors, and they do so in patterned ways. These patterns, in turn, comprise structural elements and/or enter into the production of other structural elements. For instance,

Dworkin and I (1986) argued that industrialization and urbanization served to expand the social roles available to women (structural variables). In turn, those women who experienced expanded roles tended to also experience certain social psychological problems and processes, including a shift in comparative reference group and an increasing sense of relative deprivation, which resulted in the development of gender consciousness for many (micro-level process). Finally, that consciousness, combined with new resources generated by role expansion, led to the development of a new structural element: organized women's movements.

Micro-structural gender theory provides at least part of the bridge connecting structural independent and dependent constructs. It begins by examining the ramifications of structurally induced inequities and expectations based on gender, for the behaviors of women and men. But the micro-structural approach takes as given, and therefore undertheorizes the structural elements that provide individuals with different levels of resources, and it pretty much ignores the structural ramifications of micro-level behavior. Macro-level, gender stratification theory can readily fill the first gap. The two approaches are ripe for integration, formalization, and systematic testing. Ample theoretical ideas and empirical data exist about both, which constitue a gold mine awaiting only the extraction, smelting, and shaping of their nuggets into formal theory.

The more difficult theoretical issue concerns how micro-level behaviors aggregate into structural features (in anything beyond the mere statistical sense); the micro-back-to-macro linkage. In my own recent work (1990), I attempted to deal with this issue by showing how micro-level constructs, that were behavioral in nature, produced both attitudinal and behavioral consequences which, largely through *feedback mechanisms,* were linked to structural consequences.

CONCLUSION

I am not awaiting the arrival of formally constructed theories of gender with bated breath. The problems I enumerated will not soon be solved, especially given their ideological and political overtones in the field of gender sociology. However, gender sociology is, for the several reasons enumerated, a gold mine of opportunity to develop such theory. Given the potential policy ramifications of well-developed, rigorously tested gender theory, as a feminist I believe that the effort is more than warranted. Gold doesn't disappear just because no one is mining it today. It will still be there if our discipline ever gets around to producing a sizeable number of trained miners.

Note

I am grateful for the helpful comments of Randall Collins, Helen Rose Ebaugh, and A. Gary Dworkin on an earlier draft of this paper.

9

Constructing Bridges between Sociological Paradigms and Levels: Trying to Make Sociological Theory More Complex, Less Fragmented, and Less Politicized

Jerald Hage

If our analysis about the fragmentation of sociological theory is correct—and many would agree it is correct—then any new departure in the construction of formal theory should attempt to unite disparate perspectives and specialties. Recent work in metatheory (Alexander 1982, Alender *et al*, 1987; Ritzer 1991) has asked for increased attention to unite micro and macro theories, as well as theories that assume agency and those that focus on structure. But these grandiose objectives would require no less than a Marx or at minimum a Weber if we are to offer some new grand theory. The failure of Parsons is instructive. So, a more immediate and realizable theoretical goal is to begin by integrating several different specialties within the discipline. One could start with any two or three of the combinations that are possible among the twenty some sections in the disciplines, many of which have their own conflicting perspectives. For example, rather than debate functional and conflict theory, let us start by specifying the conditions under which one or the other perspective is most appropriate. Again, integrating the new theoretical developments in rational choice theory and the sociology of emotions would provide a much more complex view of human beings than either alone. Or consider the intellectual possibilities of uniting organizational theory with governance theory in institutional economics. The examples could be multiplied endlessly, the point being that many disparate areas need to be integrated in a variety of ways.[1]

Integrating disparate specialties, however, implies a particular perspective on how to construct theories as well as on which aspects of a theory are to be emphasized. The many theory construction books published two decades ago (Stinchcombe 1968; Blalock 1969; Gibbs 1972; Hage 1972; Chafetz 1978) highlighted hypothesis construction and formalization of concepts and of measures, and in some instances even equations. With the hindsight of some twenty years, it appears to me that this strategy did not encourage synthesis because it was more concerned with explicating a particular viewpoint rather than highlighting the essential ideas in several different perspectives. In some ways, the hypothesis construction mode encouraged a kind of empiricism but one that was not concerned paradoxically with the exceptions and qualification to these hypotheses.

I propose therefore that we search for a new strategy for the construction of formal theory, one that will attempt to synthesize the various paradigms, political positions, and accumulative facts. To build bridges between specialties requires—in my view necessitates—that we focus on the fundamental assumptions of each perspective rather than the many hypotheses implied by them. We should attempt to construct deductive theory—whether in formal models or not—and at the same time, and paradoxically, we should emphasize exceptions and qualifications.

This theoretical strategy for the discipline would help reduce the problems of specialization and allow for a much more complex view of the world to be constructed, avoiding simple-minded solutions to practical problems—which is another reason why the discipline frequently looses credibility. Delineating the basic assumptions or premises furnishes a modus operandi in a discipline that is politicized because the assumptions of one theoretical perspective become the scope conditions for another. Hopefully, this will provide a constitutional principle for mutual tolerance and a basis for some intellectual progress in the discipline.

A search for exceptions and qualifications removes one of the major complaints of the feminists (see chapter 8) about the search for panhistorical generalizations because it means that one postulates the possibility that gender may be one of the most important qualifications when constructing a theory. A search for scope conditions also removes some of the major objections of many who distrust positivism. Their concerns were about the futility of searching for generalizations that could hold across time and space. But the search for conditions in a comparative historical research design quickly makes one appreciate these limits to generalizations. The work on American exceptionalism is one example and the concern for path dependent trajectories is another.

It is, however, quite simple to propose a new approach to formal theory; the difficulties lie in implementation. This chapter proposes a potential program of theory building. The definitions of what formal deductive theory and scope conditions are will be the focus of the first section. In the second section of the chapter, I sketch what might be accomplished, providing the basis of a debate about the wisdom of this particular approach. My efforts may inspire others concerned with the theoretical status of the discipline.

FORMAL DEDUCTIVE THEORY AND SCOPE CONDITIONS

What Is Formal Deductive Theory?

Theory does not have one simple and agreed upon definition, as Stinchcombe (1968) so rightly observed. Some define theory as a set of hypotheses, as did the many theory construction books written several decades ago (Hage 1972; Gibbs 1972). Others emphasize equations as in a path diagram (Blalock 1969). Still others, such as Parsons and Phils (1951), thought of typologies as theory. Still others want to focus on metatheory. Discussing a concept can be theory for still others. Consistent with the position of Cohen (1989), I propose to emphasize formal deductive theory as the key theoretical strategy to adopt when constructing theories.

There are three reasons why formal deductive theory would appear to be the best strategy at this moment in the history of the discipline. First, formal deductive theory has been the strategy of economics and, while admitting that economic reality is easier to formalize, its model of theory has proved successful. Secondly, broader and more general assumptions provide one basis for integrating across specialties and subspecialties in the discipline, and seeing similarities where none were observable previously. Thirdly, we have accumulated a large amount of knowledge since the 1960s, which has provided more opportunity for developing some broad generalizations and perceiving scope conditions as well.

One of the theoretical strengths of economic thinking is its rigor, grounded in logical deductive reasoning. Typically a theoretical economic article starts with some basic assumption and then deduces all of the many implications from it. A good example of this is micro-economics with its theory about supply and demand. The basic assumptions are quite simple: given shortages, suppliers will increase their prices and make more profit. Others will enter the market and attempt to meet the demand, thus achieving a new equilibrium between supply and demand. But the opposite is also true. Given excess capacity, some suppliers will fail and leave the market, others will lower their prices until demand increases. There is a motivational assumption underscoring it all: both suppliers and demanders want to maximize their economic gain, whether this be profits or the lowest price possible for the product.

It is not, as one might wrongly assume, the sophistication of mathematics that has empowered economics and made it impervious to various assaults but the ability to reason from first principles. Assumptions provide econo-mists with the capacity to offer policy answers for many practical problems, as we demonstrated in the awarding of the 1992 Nobel Prize to Gary Becker. Whether the answers are correct is not at issue. Deductive reasoning does allow for a flexibility of reasoning that is helpful to politicians interested in quick answers.

For our definition of formal deductive theory, the key ingredient in the laws of supply and demand is the assumption of equilibrium. The latter might be called an action law inasmuch as it predicts what will happen given a change in either supply or demand. Why the changes occur in a particular way is based on another kind of assumption, the motivational assumption about maximizing gain.

Demand and supply thinking is well known. Now, the question remains as to whether this same model of theory can be applied to sociology. Within sociology, the best example of ways of moving from hypotheses to the fun-damental assumptions that undergird them is the intellectual journey taken by Homans as he moved from the hypotheses in the *Human Group* (1950) to the assumptions in *The Elements of Social Behavior* (1961). Indeed, the latter is an exemplary demonstration of how theory can be constructed in a for-mal deductive mode. In this instance, it bears a striking resemblance to eco-nomic thinking.

Several other examples of formal deductive theory in sociology are pro-vided in table 9.1. Expectations theory is well known and has been described in a number of publications (see Cohen 1989). Here I have included the one assumption that is an action assumption since this idea may not be clear. Ex-change theory has developed a fairly consistent set of formal assumptions, building upon the work of Homans.

Also included in table 9.1 is an illustration of formal theory from my own work (Hage 1974). The example is designed to indicate how functional theory can be made predictive. Typically functional theory stopped with the first assumption about the need for order or coordination. The next step is to delineate the variety of ways in which the assumption about coordination can be obtained. Action laws then specify which of several different mechanisms are most likely to be selected.

The advantage of formal assumptions, from a policy perspective, is if some organization is lacking in coordination, then several different prescrip-tions can be provided. When the organizations are structurally differentiated, socialization should be used.

The concept of an action law is borrowed from the relatively obscure work of Bridgeman (1936); Bridgeman used the example of the planetary laws of motion. He emphasized that action laws allowed for precise predic-tions, in this case future locations. This makes them different from other

TABLE 9.1
Some Examples of Action Laws as an Ideal Explanation

Expectation State Theory

The greater the expectation that another individual with whom we are interacting will have more power or prestige, the more likely this is to occur in the interaction.[1]

Organizational Coordination and Control Theory

Functional Assumption	Organizations must coordinate to maintain effectiveness.
Mechanism Assumption	Organizations can coordinate via socialization, peer group pressure, sanctions, and programming.
Action Assumptions	As organizations become more structurally differentiated, organizations are more likely to use socialization and peer group pressures as mechanisms of coordination. As resources such as power and money become more concentrated, organizations are more likely to use sanctions and programming.
Scope Assumptions	Resource dependent organizations are unlikely to move towards the choice of socialization and peer group pressure. The longer the prior period of success with the use of sanctions and programming, the greater the resistance to adapting to socialization and group pressure.

---

1. I appreciate that I have rephrased the fourth assumption in expectation theory. My intent is to focus on the dynamic aspects; see Cohen (1989).

kinds of fundamental assumptions, as is illustrated in table 9.1. For example, if we assume that individuals like to maximize rewards in interpersonal relationships, we also need to know which rewards are most critical to which kinds of people. Some people want to maximize power, others money, and still others prestige. We need to have actions laws that stipulate which personality types (hierarchy of needs), personal histories (reward schedules), or national cultures (value preferences) and thus the specific kind of reward or outcome so as to make predictions.

The emphasis on formal deductive theory is a different theoretical strategy that Merton (Merton et al. 1959) advocated when he proposed middle-range theory in his presidential address. His theory of the role set is an example of what might be called a network theory or a set of interrelated hypotheses, the same strategy which appeared in the many theory construction books. This strategy has been widely followed by most of the specialties within sociology, as the *Annual Review of Sociology* indicates, because sociology has been a discipline that has been primarily inductive rather than deductive. Organizational theory, the sociology of education, of the family or of the military, provide good illustrations. This strategy is not objectionable as such but if we are to build bridges between these various specialties, then the discipline needs some more tightly reasoned formal deductive theory to provide the necessary dialogue to integrate several specialties.

What are Scope Conditions?

Formal deductive theory by itself will not necessarily overcome the fragmentation and politicization that have plagued sociology over the past decades. Equally important is the recognition of the limitations of our basic assumptions, in other words, their incompleteness.

In an article about the problem of contradictory findings, Walker and Cohen (1985) suggest that rather than reject theory, we should try to reformulate the theory by specifying the conditions under which one or more hypotheses hold. They do not advocate the use of other paradigms as one method for understanding negative evidence. But this is one strategy and probably the most useful one.

Again, economics provides several useful illustrations of scope conditions. Obviously, demand and supply do not always revert to equilibrium. Over time, economists have come to recognize the need for introducing qualifications. In some markets, one producer becomes dominant and consequently may not have to lower his prices, given the lack of competition.

Information about alternative products may not be known or difficult to come by. How many people know how many patients their doctor has lost? The recognition of asymmetries in information has led to a whole branch of economics called transaction costs (Williamson 1975, 1985). Not all consumers necessarily can afford the cost of a product or service, creating what is referred to as an access problem. Such imperfections in the market provide qualifications or scope conditions to the neoclassical view of the market.

The critical point in everything that precedes is that rather than treat each of these perspectives as different paradigms within economics, these perspectives are synthesized into the general paradigm. In this way economics builds theoretically rather than becoming fragmented. The consequence is that economics grows in an integrated fashion.[2]

Sociological theory could grow with the same advantages. Our assumptions have obvious limits or qualifications, that is scope conditions. For example, if we continue to use the illustrations in table 9.1, we can observe how other theories and empirical findings can be integrated into a more general framework. In the extended example from my own work, we observe that when structural differentiation occurs, a shift from one type of coordination or control mechanism to another does not automatically occur. Indeed, Lawrence and Lorsch (1967), in their theory of social integration, provide evidence of instances where this does not occur, resulting in a decrease in effectiveness measured in a variety of ways. Finally, left unanswered is *why* does the change in coordination mechanism does not occur.

Political theorists (Pfeffer 1981; Collins 1975) assume that organizations that are resource dependent or dominated by powerful elites are less able to move towards decentralization. This assumption can provide one kind of scope condition because interaction and peer socialization imply the inability of lower participants to be controlled by those in power. Furthermore, case studies demonstrate how particular occupations, when they are able to obtain power, alter the reward structure.

Institutional theory (Meyer and Rowan 1977) assumes that myths develop about organizational structures and then become institutionalized. Among the common myths, for instance, is the belief about the superiority of rewards and punishments as a mechanism for controlling the behavior of people as in many American organizations. Another is that civil service regulations prevent corruption. Somewhat different is the idea that the longer a particular structural arrangement, including the way in which individuals are controlled, is maintained successfully, the more it becomes fixed in the institutional memory of the organization and thus impervious to change.

In each instance, we have adopted another theoretical perspective to explain why organizations might not change their mechanism of coordination despite some increases in structural differentiation or complexity. The assumptions that stipulate scope conditions also have practical implications. They provide several reasons why American business has found it difficult to adjust to new competitive pressures.

The search for exceptions and qualifications is neither difficult nor time-consuming! Precisely because sociology has a complex reality and multiple origins, we will always unearth contradictory evidence and theory fragments for each action law that we attempt to formulate. But let us accept this limitation, which has led some to adopt a postmodernist skepticism about the possibility of generalization—and convert it into a source of theoretical strength. By recognizing the complexity of social reality and perceiving opportunities in disparate facts, we are given a mechanism for building bridges between different levels of analysis and different paradigms. This particular model of formal deductive theory speaks to a number of issues in a discipline such as sociology which rests upon a belief that utilities are multiple.

SOME SHORT ILLUSTRATIONS

Given the numerous doubts—many of which have been expressed in various papers in this volume—about the feasibility of formulating deductive theory, it seems incumbent upon me at least to sketch several examples of what might be accomplished with an alternative strategy of theory construction. The selections will be related to some of the major themes that are of current interest to sociologists, such as the integration of theories across levels (macro and micro), and across theories of agency and structure (subjective and objective). Accounting for the limitations of these sketches, however, is the fact that they obviously reflect current theoretical work of mine (although some of the work was done collaboratively) and therefore do not necessarily reflect some of the more exciting intellectual developments in the field. But at least they illustrate the relative effectiveness of combining assumptions from different paradigms or theoretical perspectives and indicating what might be scope conditions that specify when one or the other perspective is most relevant.

Societal Change, Role Theory, and Symbolic Interactionism

Role theory as originally formulated by Merton (1957) is a classical example of functional theory, and one that dealt with conflict. The crux of the theory placed an emphasis on role scripts, that is, the prescriptions that define what each role occupant should do. It encouraged a large amount of very good work on role conflict or disagreements about these prescriptions (see Kahn et al. 1964; Biddle 1987 for a review).

In quite a dissimilar vein Blumer (1969) and others, at about the same time, advocated a version of symbolic interactionism that allowed for negotiated order and considerable room for human agency. We are here presented with a classic example of what has produced ideological conflict in the discipline and led to its fragmentation, for the perspectives or paradigms highlight quite disparate visions of the social world. Unfortunately, because these authors placed little emphasis on explicating their basic assumptions about the nature of society and under what conditions these premises are valid, little progress was made. Indeed, I believe that over time role theory gradually lost an audience despite its empirical successes. But this says something about the kind of society that role theory implies and also the kind of society that has made symbolic interactionism as a perspective more attractive in recent years. It does not presuppose that either perspective is completely right or wrong.

Recently, Chuck Powers and I (Hage and Powers 1992) published a book that attempted to formulate which characteristics of society (and by extension sectors of society) predict the relevance of role theory or of symbolic interaction, that is, the scope conditions that would explain when one or the other theory should be applied. This work rests upon the belief that each theory is accurate and insightful only when applied to particular societies or parts of them, and specific temporal moments. In the following table are two of the

TABLE 9.2
Examples of Actions Laws Being Synthesized

Role Theory and Symbolic Interactionism

1. The larger the amount of knowledge in a society, the larger the role set and the more that the role set is coordinated via negotiated order rather than codification of role scripts.
2. The faster the rate of technological change, the more that the role set is co-ordinated via negotiated order rather than codification of role scripts.
3. The greater the inability to read symbolic communication, the greater the difficulty in negotiating role expectations, the greater the role conflict.
4. The more centralized and stratified the social institution (family, organization, market, etc.), the greater the reliance on role scripts.

Resource Mobilization and Active State

1. The greater the social and political mobilization of the industrial working class, the more that the state responds to its political agenda and pressure from the working class.
2. The stronger the state, the less it responds to the pressures of the industrial working class.
3. The less the response of the state across time, the more likely that political conflict will emerge.
4. Positive responses to the demands of the industrial working class facilitate its social and political mobilization.

Economic Market Theory and the Level of Knowledge

1. The greater the degree of competition, the more likely demand and supply will be in equilibrium.
2. The higher the level of knowledge, the less likely demand and supply will be in equilibrium.

---

main assumptions that we used; both are action laws because they specify a direction in which social change is occurring.

A useful starting point in thinking about societies in which role scripts predominate is to remember that the structural functional literature primarily builds on anthropological studies of primitive societies where ritual predominates. Furthermore, the major work on role conflict (Kahn et al. 1964) re-searched highly bureaucratized and rationalized industrial organizations where again role theory is more plausible. As many in sociology adopt a more historical perspective, role theory in its classical mode can still play an important component in their analysis. For example, feminist scholars (Clark 1984) have been examining the roles of women as depicted in textbooks used in grade schools. Such work allows one to tap much more readily into the idea of cultural hegemony; it also underscores how much role theory lies at the center of our understanding of cultural constraints. Therefore, even though role theory may appear to be irrelevant to contemporary problems in society, it does not mean it is irrelevant to theoretical issues in some specialties of the discipline.

It is also interesting to speculate about the source of Blumer's (1969) imagery. I would suggest that Blumer's idea of negotiated order reflects his middle class background and academic status, that is, conditions that allow one much more freedom of choice in role relationships. Therefore, role scripts did not appear to him to be accurate—and probably rightly so. Symbolic interactionism or more generally theories of human agency imply societies undergoing rapid sociological change because it is in them that negotiated order is most necessary. In such societies, one has to discuss and agree upon what each role partner is to do. Thus, both theories have mental images of different kinds of societies.

But what is producing a sense of considerable societal change, especially social change that impacts on roles? We suggest that where knowledge has advanced the most (assumption one) or where the rate of technological change is rapid (assumption two), then role scripts are likely to be abandoned and negotiated order will prevail. Explicitly, we posit an evolutionary theory arguing that across time, Blumer's vision is likely to become the predominant one. In other terms, in industrial society, role theory is the most useful paradigm while in postindustrial society, symbolic interaction is more informative. Since knowledge advances at dissimilar rates in various sectors of society, these same assumptions can explain how role theory is still a useful perspective for parts of society.

Does this make role theory irrelevant in the society of the future? Each perspective develops analytical concepts that are likely to be abandoned as we move from one set of theoretical problems or fashionable ideas or problem to the next. Even if our argument is correct about the contemporary relevance of symbolic interaction as a perspective, it does not mean that all the knowledge that has accumulated in role theory is worthless. Yet this is implied by the lack of references to role theory (Biddle 1987) and illustrates how little accumulation of knowledge there is.

We believe that two major ideas in role theory must be retained and employed in contemporary symbolic interactionism: role sets as collections of role relationships and role conflict about expectations within these role sets. In our book, we argue that growth in knowledge is forcing the size of the role set to expand more or less continuously, gradually elaborating into social networks. It is this phenomenon that has made network analysis so vital in present-day sociology. But this same expansion in the size of role sets— therein lies the theoretical irony—has led to a considerable increase in role conflict as manifested in the divorce rates in the United States as well as the number of studies of work stress. Given conflicts about expectations in large role sets, negotiating who will do what, when and where becomes the dominant mode. Complex role sets cannot be managed by role scripts. In short, Merton (1968) had the right concept, while Blumer (1969) had the best intuition about the future. Furthermore, the concept of role set also leads us naturally to what is a major new area of research, namely networks, providing another, very necessary bridge between specialties.

Basic assumptions focus on theoretical attention on concepts much more effectively than do a variety of hypotheses. If we retain the idea of role sets, especially as a collection of role relationships, then we need to develop variables for describing them besides the obvious idea of a complex or large role set. Hage and Powers (1992), building upon the previous work of Hage and Marwell (1969), have suggested one set of variables for analyzing role relationships and, by extension, role sets. With these a number of ideas can be generated.

One advantage of synthesizing the basic assumptions of different perspectives or specialties is that it allows us to gain insights relative to practical problems in the society. Clearly, the large divorce rate and its consequences for children have become major issues in the newspapers and magazines, and for a number of good reasons. Children are living in poverty, teenage pregnancies have sky-rocketed, school drop-out rates are common among children in single-parent families, and other signs of distress are observable. What distinctive insights can sociological theory contribute to this set of problems?

Our premises suggest that while there has been a shift from role scripts to negotiated order, most people appear incapable of handling negotiation. Blumer (1969) did not treat this as problematic, assuming that order would emerge. In this sense, Blumer (1969) exhibited the same optimism as Merton (1968), who focused on how various kinds of mechanisms dampened role conflict. Instead, successful negotiation would appear to be the exception rather than the general pattern, not just in family role relationships but in the gridlock of the American political system, the ethnic conflict of former Yugoslavia, and a variety of other examples of breakdown. Furthermore, Blumer did not anticipate the complexity of having to negotiate expectations in large role sets, rather than in single role relationships (more common in the 1950s).

If we examine family roles and their role sets for instance, we find that increased complexity is the result of women adding work roles and their associated activities while men are being asked to fulfill family roles as well as the various obligations associated with these. Nowadays, men and women are finding it difficult to alter their expectations in these contexts. Beyond this, the variables for describing role relationships indicate that a number of other kinds of changes have been producing stress in the role set of parents. The line of reasoning, which is after all a very simple assumption, then begins to shed light on some ideas about how to ameliorate social problems. In one sense, this is a test of the usefulness of the assumptions as well as an indication of how sociology can be made relevant to the larger world.

In our book *Post-Industrial Lives* (1992) we also observe that in rapidly changing societies, role transformation is becoming the norm. But with family roles tending to be negotiated at a single point of time, the social contracts are not reconsidered until it is too late. For if social change becomes a constant, then by definition, negotiation over the social contracts must be a constant as well. Again, this was not really part of the original imagery of Blumer.

Since symbolic interactionism assumes that negotiated order does prevail, the search for scope conditions leads naturally to inquiry under what circumstances people *fail* to negotiate. By defining symbolic interaction as the ability to discern both verbal and nonverbal messages, then we can appreciate that individuals who are unable to bargain about role expectations successfully are those that can not read symbolic communication. In the book *Post-Industrial Lives* (Hage and Powers 1992) our analysis of symbolic communication allows us to unite cognitive theories such as role theory and symbolic interactionism with the new theory of emotions. Nonverbal messages are primarily emotional news about the importance attached by the speaker to his/her message whether or not the speaker believes in what he or she is saying, the specific emotive content, and finally the relative importance of the audience or role partner to the speaker. Each of these messages helps to solve a fundamental issue in social psychology such as the capacity of the speaker to motivate others, the problem of the double bind, realization of self and social connections or feelings of belonging, and so forth. This is another test of the worth of basic assumptions and concepts: they should integrate major theoretical issues in the specialty.

We could also specify other scope conditions. Society or sectors of it may change but, within particular families or organizations, roles can still be prescribed. The debate about family values in the 1992 election campaign reflected essentially a desire to return to traditional roles for men and women. As we have suggested, an important intellectual source for contingencies is located in other paradigms. For example, one could borrow from Collins's (1975) theory of power differentials leading to deference and thus the creation of role scripts, an idea also involved in organizational theory (Hage 1980). Centralized and stratified families are likely to have carefully prescribed role scripts; aristocratic families are one example. Similarly, centralized and bureaucratic organizations will use role prescriptions, the Catholic church is an illustration. Again, we have an example of how the scope conditions are frequently located on other levels of analysis, in this instance the meso level.

Resource Mobilization Theory versus the Strong State

A direct implication of Marx's theory about the growth of the industrial working class is the thesis that when the industrial working class is mobilized, it is able to put pressure on the state and achieve many of its demands despite the opposition of the capitalist class (Stephens 1979; Korpi 1989). The opposing perspective is that states can be strong and resist pressures from the working class (Orloff and Skocpol 1984; Amenta and Carruthers 1988; Quadango 1987), and pursue their own strategies. These two assumptions take the original idea of Marx about the dialectic between the classes and suggest instead that the more fundamental dialectic is between classes (or perhaps ways in which people are mobilized) and the state (or perhaps the predominant social institutions in the society at a particular historical moment).

The implied resolution of these two assumptions can be combined in still a third assumption, which argues that the nonresponsiveness of the state leads eventually to the emergence of social (street demonstrations, riots, major strikes) and political (emergence of new parties, general strikes, armed rebellion) conflict about the needs that are not being addressed. Thus, strong states are eventually corrected via processes of vote shifts, the emergence of third and radical parties, and finally revolution. Nor does state resistance to pressures from the working class provide the only source of mobilization. The middle class during the Progressive Era in the United States felt trapped between powerful labor unions and the capitalist class, and proceeded to reform the political system so that it could not as easily be captured by either group, hence our system of primaries and attempts to prevent the purchase of votes. Again, more recently, the capitalist class mobilized during the late 1970s and helped push Reagan into the presidency (Clawson et al. 1992)

Although we have not attached any assumptions about the demands of other social classes, these could be easily added to the model as variations on the same theme; with the inclusion of each class, we would want to specify as much as possible the preferred utilities of each of these groups (see Hollingsworth 1986) because they indicate the kinds of class dialectics at work as well as possible class compromises or alliances. With these more detailed assumptions, we could begin to analyze the political equilibrium that is established between the demands of the working class, middle class, and capitalist class and the supply of the state (for empirical analyses of these ideas see Hage, Hanneman, and Gargan 1989). Since each class/interest group makes distinct demands, there are constraints on what the state can provide, ensuring the existence of a political dynamic across time (O'Connor 1973). These authors have outlined a theory about the endless sources of societal change within the political system—assuming some form of democratic rule. But the same theory can analyze nondemocratic rule as well by observing that very strong states can resist demands until they lose all legitimacy, as occurred in the former Soviet Union, leading to sudden collapse, due to dissatisfaction among almost all classes/interest groups in society. It is then that radical institutional change becomes possible.

One of the advantages of focusing on action laws as a particular kind of assumption is that the theorist is led immediately to speculate about which conditions influence the mobilization of the working class, other classes, and interest groups, and therefore to consider various potential scope conditions.[3] For example, in this particular instance, one critical factor is the relevance of social dimensions upon which categories of people can be mobilized (e.g., gender, race, ethnicity, religion, etc.). When there exists a wide variety of ways in which individuals can be mobilized in a society, then the mobilization of the working class becomes more problematic. One illustration is the importance of the Catholic religion in Europe, which has been stressed by many commentators (Stephens 1979; Esping-Andersen 1990).

Another form of a dual scope condition is the relative size of each class and the number of social classes. The United States has had a relatively simple, one might even say classical, class structure: A working class, a middle class, and a capitalist class. Furthermore, the middle class is large and not sharply defined. Specific key elements in the history of this country are the absence of an aristocracy (except in the South) and a peasant class (again except in the South). Given the relatively large middle class and a large capitalist class, especially if we include entrepreneurs in this category, then the natural coalition will be formed between these two classes against the working class, making it difficult for this class to gain power. In addition, in the United States, the existence of racial, ethnic, and religious distinctions further weakens the power of the working class since the politicians can undermine the solidarity of the working class by dividing electoral appeals along these lines. Knowing how a society's class structure is configured historically allows us to understand a great deal about its specific pathway of evolution.

Knowing how states are organized also tells us something about the internal strength of a state to resist pressures. Clearly, if the power is concentrated in an administrate elite, as it is in some countries, the state will be much stronger (Hage, Hanneman, and Gargan 1989). But specific conditions can prevail that alter the strength of the state. For example, if the state is controlled by a military junta, then it is likely to be much stronger. The absence of democratic elections and choices between candidates also strengthens the state, although only for the short span of a generation or two. If the elite is selected on the basis of quite rigorous exams, then the civil service is more likely to have legitimacy; a competent civil service implies the ability to solve problems, therefore conferring legitimacy upon the state. In turn, the inability to solve problems mobilizes groups into social movements (civil rights, equal rights, Townsden movement, consumer movement, etc.) as we have seen frequently in the United States. The Green movement is only one of the most contemporary examples of such mobilization in Europe.

However, as everyone is aware, the dynamics of class demands versus state actions is much more complicated than these three assumptions imply. Therefore, we must begin to search for exceptions and qualifications to these basic assumptions. One can begin this task by identifying scope conditions that would indicate when relatively weak states do not respond to mobilized working classes. First, one kind of scope condition would be the relative power of the middle or capitalist class. Even with strong and well-mobilized working classes, high mobilization of the middle class, especially if the class structure results in an alliance of the middle and the capitalist class, prevents the working class from gaining power. Even a powerful working class would find it difficult to receive much from the state under these circumstances, as illustrated in the case of the United States.

Second, at an extreme, the state becomes so weak that it can not respond to any kind of class pressure, whether this be the working, middle, or capitalist class. The society may be fragmented into a number of different classes, even though the working class is itself well-mobilized, which will prevent any uniform attack on the social and political problems of the society. Italy provides an example of this class/institutional dialectic.

Third, one can ask, when do strong states respond to poorly mobilized classes? Strong states can adopt a policy of intervening on the side of the working class against the capitalist class. If the aristocracy controls the state, this is likely to happen when it is hostile to the growth in power of the capitalist class. In the process, the mobilization of the working class is facilitated, changing the direction of the working class and the institutional evolution within the society. Germany is an example of this class/institutional dialectic.

I have added as a fourth assumption that positive state responses facilitate the processes of political and social mobilization because it allows us to understand how early in the processes of industrialization some working-class movements gained strength—as they did in Germany and England. In contrast, when the state refuses to respond to working-class demands, the working-class movements remained relatively weak as they did in France. If the state continues to intervene on the side of the capital during strike actions or fails to pass social legislation, then the working-class movement is likely to be fragmented along political lines (revolution vs. evolution) and never grow. Thus this fourth assumption allows us to understand how societies evolve across time.

Degree of Competition, Level of Knowledge, and the Laws of Supply and Demand

Dual labor market theory in sociology distinguishes between competitive markets, usually involving small business, and oligopolistic markets, where there is a high degree of economic concentration. Empirical evidence supporting the existence of two markets has *not* been strong; a number of studies have suggested that there is a variety of factors that appear to interact with the dynamics (Hodson and Kaufman 1982; Baron and Bielby 1980; Kallenberg and Berg 1988). Economics also has worked with one model of the market place and with one major exception, the monopoly market. But again a careful review of the evidence (Scherer 1980) indicates that the patterns are not so simple; sometimes monopolies are innovative, sometimes not.

Much more sense of the empirical findings can be made when the dimension "degree of competition," which describes the differences between the competitive and oligopolistic markets, is cross-classified with another dimension: the degree of investment in knowledge—education, research and development, and sophisticated technologies. The more knowledge that is invested in the market—that is the competing firms use high technology, whether small or large—the faster the rate of technological change is and obviously the less likely demand and supply can regain equilibrium. Knowledge also directly influences the level of competition by reducing the number of competitors via the process of generating market niches. Education has a similar impact because more educated people prefer specialized, high-quality products provided with a large amount of customer service. As White (1981) has argued, quality niches exist in many product markets, which also reduces competition among firms.

However, the laws of supply and demand break down in high-tech markets for other reasons. In several articles (Hage 1989, 1990), I have suggested that educated consumers do not respond to constraints on their pocketbook by shifting to cheaper products but maintain brand loyalty. Managers of high-tech firms appreciate that the core technology is located in the brains of their researchers and professional and technical staff. Therefore, even with declining sales, they attempt to maintain their employees and even provide raises to prevent them from changing jobs. All of these consumer and managerial behaviors cut the linkage between demand and supply and explain why the Phillips curve has shifted to the right.

Here is an example of where sociological insight is employed to establish scope conditions for economic assumptions rather than to borrow economic ideas in order to explain sociological behavior.

CONCLUSIONS

Our social engineering program for creating a more unified discipline in sociology and synthesizing specialties rests on moving up from the level of hypotheses to the level of assumptions and then indicating the scope conditions. Unlike hypotheses—which tend to be quite specific—broad-based assumptions are much easier to reason with and help us recognize both how they might be combined with other paradigms or perspectives, as well as define their limitations. It is the simplicity and generality of premises or assumptions that recommend them!

The three very short examples provided in this paper of how one can combine different paradigms by recognizing that each has particular kinds of scope conditions, hopefully suggest the advantages of building bridges between different perspectives. Not only does integration appear to be facilitated, but so does the search for practical solutions to basic problems, as we have indicated with our first example and could have done so with the others, especially the last one.

The basic assumptions also help us organize our thoughts about how to proceed to extend the theory and focus our attention on the critical concepts. By being sparse and abstract, our theoretical ideas have a better chance to grow in multiple directions.

Part III
Implications for the Discipline

10

Recommendations from Jerald Hage

When the American Sociological Association provided the money for the conference, they hoped that the fruits of the conference would be shared with the larger discipline. Throughout, and especially in the introductory remarks for each part, I have stressed what appear to be the implicit debates that emerge from the papers. Hopefully, one outcome of publishing this book, will be an extended debate among graduate students and the young faculty about the best theoretical approach to the problems of the discipline. Clearly, what kinds of formal theory should be emphasized is one important issue for extended discussion.

But at various points a number of other implications emerge. Below are two short essays that make a series of recommendations about how graduate programs might be altered. In chapter 8 Chafetz suggests a major change in the nature of theory courses that are taught, an issue that also emerges in Blalock's contribution (chapter 7). In both instances, these are recommendations for the need to connect theory and research, a theme that was touched upon in the introduction to the second section and the discussion of formal theory.

Actions at the Departmental Level

If one accepts the idea that there have been too much specialization and fragmentation within various sociology departments, then one recommendation for reducing these tendencies is to have each department, depending upon its size, emphasize only two specialties per ten faculty members. In this way, one can achieve both coherence and diversity. This implies a change in the nature of recruitment; rather than emphasize the best person that is available, recruitment must attempt to build strengths in specific areas. To build theory, regardless of what kind and in what areas, we need to have concentrations of people within departments so that more complex theories that are oriented towards solving problems—whether theoretical or applied—become possible. Many departments have already achieved a considerable amount of focus, which will improve the integration of the discipline in the long term.

If a department is politicized, then one possibility for reducing the degree of fractionization somewhat is to search for candidates that bridge the different specialties that are in conflict. This is an old idea from sociology—overlapping status sets—and an important way in which integration is accomplished in business organizations (Lawrence and Lorsch 1967). Finding effective middle women or men is not always possible, but surely any efforts that are made to reduce internal conflict means freeing energy that can then be applied to advancing the discipline.

Still another variation on the theme of reducing fragmentation is to combine narrow specialties into broader areas. Emory combines political economy and development into one area. Maryland has joined organizations, occupations, and labor markets into one comprehensive area. *Contemporary Sociology* has been suggesting a number of combinations that provide more breath and yet do not demand too much. How specialty or comprehensive areas are defined speaks to how students study and how they think. Typically departments have either allowed too much narrow specialization or asked for too broad a comprehensive exam (such as social organization). The idea is to combine several paradigms or perspectives within the same specialty area as well as several specialties.

Consistent with this reorganization of the exams, the courses that prepare students for these exams should be taught by different faculty so as to introduce varying perspectives and paradigms. For example, if the examination topic is in development, one course could emphasize the world systems perspective and another the modernization paradigm. Again, this is likely to encourage students to think about the scope conditions of these alternative theories about the world.

Actions for the American
Sociological Association

There are a number of small steps that can be taken in the ASA to encourage the development of new theories and the accumulation of knowledge. For example, the theory section could do so by allocating one of its annual sessions to new theories, leaving aside questions of area or generality. The ASA itself can take stock of knowledge in particular areas by sponsoring one conference a year in a different specialty area where the attempt is made to assess what is known, to create new theories, and to explicate what needs to be done next, as a collective effort. Here, recent developments in social psychology provide a model.

I appreciate that this is what the *Annual Review of Sociology* is supposed to accomplish, but because reviews are written by a single author—or an author and her/his student—I believe that many of the essays fail to achieve this collective assessment of what is known and what is not known. Conferences appear to be a more effective method for achieving theory assessment and building precisely because one needs four to six people for these tasks. Theory building conferences are also worth setting up as a way of generating new theories that span some of the narrow specialties contained in the groupings used in *Contemporary Sociology*. Let me suggest that a conference on how to integrate occupational and organizational theories would be fruitful. Another potentially interesting topic for such a gathering would synthesize class and feminist theories. Still a third example, is a conference on uniting cognitive theories and the sociology of emotions. The various attempts at synthesis in chapter 9 represent additional illustrations of topics worthy of a conference. The potentialities are endless and their collective products would help reduce conflict at the departmental level.

Especially important could be encouraging theoretical work on the development of new paradigms via the synthesis of old ones. Above, in chapter 9, I tried to provide several examples. Evolutionary theory might be one area in which a number of theoretical perspectives could be combined. Likewise the game-theoretic approach to social interaction suggested by Abell (chapter 6) may be another.

Also, the ASA might want to encourage the development of more deductive theory that spans several levels (micro, meso, and macro) or institutional sectors (welfare and education). This would create a dialectic and encourage theorists to move beyond their narrow specialty. On the other hand, I would not encourage attempting to develop a grand theory for all of sociology as Turner suggests in the next section. My prescription is for neither middle-range theory nor "grand" theory, but instead the integration of several adjacent paradigms and/or specialty areas.

Similarly, rather than one author writing a theory construction book, suppose that the ASA commissioned a synthetic effort in the form of a book written by several people, thus hopefully combining strengths and reducing weaknesses of previous efforts. Perhaps a multifaceted book that reflected multiple levels of analyses would have more impact on the discipline, especially on the behavior of sociologists. Certainly, it would be important to include in such a work sensitivity to qualitative and/or historical theory as well as theory found in particular segments of society. Another important advantage would accrue if some chapters written by a team involving one theorist and one methodologist or statistician. In other words, if we are to create more complex theories, we need more complex approaches to formal theory than were suggested some twenty years ago and we probably need teams working together.

In sum, the major prescription for the discipline is to create opportunities for more dialogue between the disparate specialties with the hope of facilitating more effective problem solving theory as requested by both Gibbs and Cohen.

Notes

1. Some people resist synthesizing theories since they believe that the purity of the original ideas lost. How much this is true depends upon the way in which the theories are connected. A contingency theory approach reduces the amount of alteration of the original, instead indicating the scope conditions when the theory is operative or applicable.

2. This is not to say that economics does not also have its quarrels, for example the general debate between Keynesians and monetarists.

3. Another advantage is that it also allows one to consider quite carefully the problem of how to measure such basic concepts as the mobilization of the working class and the strength of the state. In other words, one test of the centrality of the ideas is whether they locate fundamental conceptual issues in the literature.

11

Recommendations by Jonathan Turner

In chapter 2, I presented a most pessimistic view on the prospects for scientific sociology in general and formal theorizing in particular. This view emphasized that sociology has failed to institutionalize formal theorizing *across the whole discipline,* while at the same time recognizing that creative formal theorizing has been practiced in various specialized intellectual niches. The basic problem, then, is not the lack of good theory; rather it is the inability of theory to define the research problems of the discipline and to cumulate a corpus of accepted knowledge as a result of systematic assessment at the empirical level and synthesis at the conceptual level. For in the discipline as a whole, it will be difficult for theory to overcome the centrifugal forces of an intellectual enterprise that cannot (*a*) exclude the lay public's claim to equal knowledge, (*b*) prevent competing organizations from entering its intellectual turf, (*c*) control reputational credits and material resources, (*d*) reduce task uncertainty by clear definitions of problems, or (*e*) foster mutual dependence and mechanisms of control in organizing the activities of knowledge-producers. Are matters hopeless? And is sociology indeed "the impossible science," as Steven Park Turner and I once proclaimed (Turner and Turner 1990)? Let me offer some ideas on what might be done to improve theorizing *and* its institutionalization within a disciplinary organizational structure that is not well suited to developing cumulative knowledge.

DEMONSTRATING THE POWER OF FORMAL THEORY THROUGH COLONIZATION OF RESEARCH SUBFIELDS

In light of the past and current organizational structure of sociology, formal theorizing will only have a widely felt impact on sociology by *demonstrating* its superiority over alternative forms of producing knowledge. The "proof will be in the pudding," and so, theorists cannot continue to argue at an

176

epistemological level only with each other but rather they must take their formal theories into sociology's specific empirical subfields and show scholars what formal theory can do. Such efforts cannot be one-time events, but they must be concerted, persistent, and long-term engagements with researchers in a subfield.

In some subfields, this demonstration strategy has already worked rather well. For example, the study of organizations is impregnated with theory; and it is probably our most sophisticated subfield because many research problems are guided by theory and because intellectual discourse revolves around which theories best explain organizational process. What is true within the study of organizations is also evident to a degree in other specialties—for example, collective behavior and social movements, ethnic conflict, stratification, and social change/development/modernization. Other subfields can similarly be penetrated by formal theory which can demonstrate how research can be better interpreted, organized, and conducted. Indeed, I suspect that many empirical subfields are ripe, if not desperate, for explanatory theories because they have reached the limit of their descriptive capacity (i.e., how many more empirical studies can members of that field find interesting?).

This demonstration strategy requires entrepreneurship—actively going out and hustling empirical literatures and their producers, and then, convincing them that they are better off with a general theory. Indeed, as general theories begin to compete over the interpretation of research, the less viable theories will be weeded out. If only a few theories survive such competition the tendency for theory-proliferation in sociology would be arrested; and perhaps serious efforts to consolidate the remaining theories would ensue.

ORGANIZED RESEARCH PROGRAMS

Some of the most creative formal theorizing in sociology currently comes from organized research programs where scholars at a university or relatively small set of universities conduct research and train students within a narrow theoretical tradition. Such efforts produce on a more miniscale the conditions for successful cumulation of knowledge—that is, excluding the lay public and competing knowledge producers, consolidating control over reputation credits and resources, fostering mutual dependence, and lowering task uncertainty over what is important.

The best exemplar of this approach is the development of "expectation states" theory at Stanford University (e.g., Berger and Zelditch 1985; Berger, Wagner, and Zelditch 1989). As a prestigious university, Stanford can recruit and place high-quality students who then can continue to recruit and place further cohorts of students. Over time, this process has created relatively dispersed but intellectually dense network of scholars at prestigious universities, a good many of whom work on variants of the theory as they learned it. In this way, a theory can grow and proliferate, and then be consolidated, by scholars who share certain common starting points and assumptions. Moreover, diverse research activities will focus on the growth of the theory and, thereby, not drive a wedge between research and theory nor proliferate research in so many diverse directions that it loses coherence (Wagner and Berger 1985).

Other organized research programs—for example, ethnomethodology out of UCLA, world systems analysis out of SUNY–Binghamton, organizational ecology out of the informal consortium among Stanford, Berkeley, and Cornell—are further illustrations of how coherent (if not always formal) theory can be produced as a result of the intellectual and organizational dynamics of research groups. Yet, these examples also illustrate the limitations of this approach to building cumulative theory in sociology. What often occurs is the institutionalization of a theory or research "camp" at a set of universities which come to have little interest in scholarly theoretical work outside of their camp. Ethnomethodology has certainly gone this way as conversational analysts address primarily each other; similarly, world systems theorists and human ecologists have, with some exceptions, also become somewhat parochial, with little effort to build bridges to other theory-research traditions.

Thus, organized research groups can produce ever more general theory—as is illustrated by the Stanford school—but they can also create new intellectual divisions and partitions which operate to fragment theory and research. The key to organized research groups is for them to be not only entrepreneurial, but they must also be imperialistic and march out from their camp in an effort to explain an ever wider range of social phenomena. Such theoretical imperialism will, of course, eventually confront another imperialistic theory group, but such clashes can perhaps prove useful *if* (and this is a problematic "if") the conflict is over the explanatory power theories and their capacity to explain research traditions. Out of these contests can come reconciliation, accommodation, and synthesis of theories—all of which can produce better theory that has a chance of cutting across all the diverse specialties of contemporary sociology.

ARMCHAIR AND GRAND THEORIZING

Ever since C. Wright Mills' (1959) famous attack on "grand theory," efforts at developing armchair and grand theories have been viewed with suspicion in American sociology. Instead, following Merton's (1968) pleas for "middle range" theory, sociology has many "theories of" empirical phenomena in each specialized subfield, a process that has legitimated and encouraged the partitioning of sociology in ways that discourage theoretical cumulation through conceptual synthesis.

Perhaps it is self-serving, but I would like to close my assessment of what can be done to develop cumulative theory in sociology with a defense of grand theory. Contrary to Alexander's (1988) and others' insistence on working within theoretical traditions, I believe that efforts at developing theories that cut across traditions and that incorporate a wide array of "middle range" theories is one way to re-institutionalize theorizing. Such grand theories should seek to synthesize existing theories and incorporate a broad range of research findings. These grand theories can be stated formally, but in ways that attract scholars rather than repel them. My best sense of how this can be done is through abstractions—whether represented as text, propositions, or models—that are copiously illustrated with examples and references to research literatures (this latter activity being the great deficiency in my own attempts at grand theory). For without this attachment of theory to the research interests of a subfield as it is presently constituted, grand theories will be read by other grand theorists, and few others.

But without grand, general, formal, and abstract theories, sociology cannot become a unified discipline. There are many structural-organizational obstacles to grand theory, but unless some try to develop such theories and to demonstrate their relevance to specialists, sociology will indeed remain "the impossible science" (Turner and Turner 1990). Sociology can become the "possible science" if general, armchair theorists can formulate their theories in ways that appeal both to researchers and fellow theorists—not an easy task. Yet, in the end, this is exactly what must be done, not only by grand theorists but also by those in organized research groups.

We must all seek a delicate balance between being general and relevant to specialists, being abstract and yet sufficiently empirical, and being formal and still communicative to the vast majority of sociologists. I do not advocate a compromise to the vacuous middle range, but a renewed effort to be general and grand as well as abstract and formal in ways that intrigue researchers and co-opt more specialized theories. This call has few organization supports, and so, we must do it alone by the power of our ideas and the capacity to communicate to a wide audience.

Reference List

Abbott, A. 1984, "Event Sequence and Event Duration: Colligation and Measurement," *Historical Methods* 17, 4:192–204.

Abbott, A. 1990, "Conceptions of Time and Events in Social Science Methods." *Historical Methods*, 23. No 4:140–150.

Abbott, A. and J. Forrest 1986, "Optimal Matching Methods for Historical Sequences." *Journal of Interdisciplinary History, XVI*, 3:471–494.

Abbott, A. and J. Forrest 1988, "Transcending General Linear Reality." *Sociological* Theory, 6:169–186.

Abell, P. 1988, The " 'Structuration of Action' " Inference and Comparative Narratives, in *Actions and Structure*, (ed.) Nigel G. Fielding, London Sage.

Abell, P. 1989, *The Syntax of Social Life, the Theory and Method of Comparative Narratives*, OUP, Oxford.

Abell, Peter. (ed.) 1991. Rational Choice Theory Brookfield.

Abell, Peter 1987 The Syntax of Social Life: The Theory and Method of Comparative narratives Clarendon Press, NY

Abelson, Robert P. 1963. "A 'Derivation' of Richard's Equations." *Journal of Conflict Resolution* 7: 13–15.

Alexander, Alexander, et al. 1987. *The Micro-Macro Link*. Berkeley, CA: University of California Press.

Alexander, Jeffrey C. 1982, 1983. Theoretical Logic in Sociology. 4 vols. Berkeley, CA: University of California Press.

———. 1988. "The New Theoretical Movement." in Neil J. Smelser (ed.) *Handbook of Sociology*. Newbury Park, CA: Sage.

Alford, Robert, and Roger Friedland. 1985. *Powers of Theory.* Cambridge, MA: Cambridge University Press.

Alter, Cathy, and Jerald Hage. 1993. *Organizations Working Together.* Newbury Park, CA: Sage.

Amenta, Edwin, and Bruce Carruthers. 1988. ''The Formative Years of U.S. Social Spending Policies.'' *American Sociological Review* 53 (August: 661–78.

Analyzing Social Interaction: Advances in Affect Control Theory. 1988. (ed) Smith-Lovin, L. and David R. Heise, Gordon and Breach Science Publishers, NY

Ashley, W. Graham, and Andrew Van de Ven. 1983. ''Central Perspectives in Debates in Organization Theory.'' *Administrative Science Quarterly* 28:245–73.

Axelrod, Robert. 1984. *The Evolution of Cooperation* New York: Basic Books.

Bacharach, Samuel B., and Edward J. Lawler. 1981. *Bargaining, Power, Tactics, and Outcomes.* San Francisco: Jossey-Bass.

Baron, James, and William Biebly. 1980. ''Bringing the Firm Back In: Stratification, Segmentation and the Organization of Work.'' *American Sociological Review* 45:737–65.

Berger, Joseph, Bernard P. Cohen, and Morris Zelditch, Jr. 1966. ''Status Characteristics and Expectation States.'' In Joseph Berger, Morris Zelditch, Jr. and Bo Anderson (eds.), *Sociological Theories in Progress.* Vol. 1., Boston: Houghton-Mifflin.

Berger, Joseph, Thomas L. Conner, and M. Hamit Fisek. 1974. *Expectation States Theory: A Theoretical Research Program.* Cambridge, MA: Winthrop.

Berger, Joseph, M. Hamit Fisek, Robert Z. Norman, and Morris Zelditch, Jr. 1977. *Status Characteristics and Social Interaction: An Expectation States Approach.* New York: Elsevier.

Berger, Joseph, David G. Wagner, and Morris Zelditch, Jr. 1983. *Expectation States Theory: The Status of a Research Program.* Technical report no. 90, Stanford University.

Berger, Joseph and Morris Zelditch, Jr. (eds.). 1985. *Status, Rewards and Influence: How Expectations Organize Behavior.* San Francisco: Jossey-Bass.

Berger, Joseph, David Wagner, and Morris Zelditch. 1989. "Theory Growth, and Social Processes, and Methatheory." In J. H. Turner (ed.) *Theory Building in Sociology.* Newbury Park, CA: Sage.

Biddle, Bruce. 1987. "Recent Developments in Role Theory." *Annual Review of Sociology* 12:67–92.

Blalock, Hubert M. Jr. 1969. *Theory Construction.* Englewood Cliffs, NJ: Prentice Hall.

———. 1982. *Conceptualization and Measurement in the Social Sciences.* Beverly Hills, CA: Sage.

———. 1986. "Multiple Causation, Indirect Measurement and Generalizability in the Social Sciences." *Synthese* 68:13–36.

———. 1989a. *Power and Conflict: Toward a General Theory.* Newbury Park, CA: Sage.

———. 1989b. "The Real and Unrealized Contributions of Quantitative Sociology." *American Sociological Review* 54:447–60.

———. Forthcoming. "Creating Opportunities for Disciplined Creativity." *Teaching Sociology.*

Blau, Peter M. 1972. "Status Characteristics and Social Interaction." *American Sociological Review* 37:241–55.

———. 1989. "Structures of Social Positions and Structures of Social Relations." In Jonathan H. Turner (ed.), *Theory Building in Sociology.* Newbury Park, CA: Sage.

Blau, Peter M., and Joseph E. Schwartz. 1984. *Crosscutting Social Circles.* Orlando, FL: Academic Press.

Blumberg, Rae 1984 A General Theory of Gender Stratification in Randal Collins (ed) *Sociological Theory* San Francisco, CA Jossey-Bass.

Blumberg, Rae Lesser. 1984. "A General Theory of Gender Stratification." In R. Collins (ed.), *Sociological Theory.* San Francisco: Jossey-Bass.

————. 1988. "Income under Female versus Male Control: Hypotheses from a Theory of Gender Stratification and Data from the Third World." *Journal of Family Issues* 9:51–84.

Blumer, H. 1969. *Symbolic Interactionism.* Englewood Cliffs, NJ: Prentice Hall.

Boudon, Raymond 1981 *The Logic of Social Action.* (translated by David Silverman) London: Routledge and Kegan Paul.

Bourdieu, Pierre. 1984, 1988. *Homo Academicus.* Stanford: Stanford University Press.

Bridgeman, Percy W. 1936. *The Nature of Physical Theory.* New York: Dover.

Burawoy, Michael. 1990. "Marxism as Science." *American Sociological Review* 55:775–93.

Chafetz, Janet S. 1978. *A Primer on the Construction and Testing of Theories in Sociology.* Itasca, IL: Peacock.

————. 1984. *Sex and Advantage: A Comparative, Macro-Structural Theory of Sex Statification.* Totowa, NJ: Rowman and Allanheld.

————. 1988. *Feminist Sociology: An Overview of Contemporary Theories.* F. E. Peacock (ed). Itasca, IL.

————. 1989. "And the Walls Come Tumbling Down: Enriching the Sociology of Gender by Systematically Using Other Disciplines." *The American Sociologist,* Summer, 160–69.

————. 1990. *Gender Equity: A Theory of Stability and Change.* Newbury Park, CA: Sage.

Chafetz, Janet S., and A. Gary Dworkin. 1986. *Female Revolt: Women's Movements in World and Historical Perspective.* Totowa, NJ: Rowman and Allanheld.

Chambliss, William J., and Robert B. Seidman. 1971. *Law, Order and Power.* Reading, MA: Addison-Wesley.

Chodorow, Nancy. 1979. *The Reproduction of Mothering: Psychoanalysis and the Sociology of Gender.* Berkeley, CA: University of California Press.

Clark, Linda. 1984. *Schooling the Daughters of Mairanne: Textbooks and the Sociologization of Girls in Modern French Primary Schools.* Albany: State University of New York Press.

Clawson, Donald, Alan Neustadtl, and Denise Scott. 1992. *Money Talks.* New York: Basic Books.

Cohen, Bernard P. 1989. *Developing Sociological Knowledge: Theory and Method.* 2nd ed. Chicago: Nelson-Hall.

———. 1980. "The Conditional Nature of Scientific Knowledge." In Lee Freese (ed.), *Theoretical Methods in Sociology: Seven Essays.* Pittsburgh, PA: University of Pittsburgh Press.

Cohen, Elizabeth G. Forthcoming. "From Theory to Practice: The Development of an Applied Research Program." In J. Berger and M. Zelditch (eds.), *Theoretical Research Programs.* Stanford, CA: Stanford University Press.

Coleman, James S. 1990. *Foundations of Social Theory.* Cambridge, MA: Harvard University Press.

Collins, Randall. 1975. *Conflict Sociology: Toward an Explanatory Science.* New York: Academic Press.

———. 1984. "Statistics versus Words." *Sociological Theory 1984.* San Francisco: Jossey-Ball.

———. 1988. "Women and Men in the Class Structure." *Journal of Family Issues* 9 (1):27–50.

————. 1989. "Sociology Proscience or Antiscience." *American Sociological Review* 54:124–39.

Comte, Auguste. 1830–1842. *The Positive Philosophy of Auguste Comte.* 3 vols. London: George Bell.

Cook, Judith A., and Mary Margaret Fonow. 1986. "Knowledge and Women's Interests: Issues of Epistemology and Methodology in Feminist Sociological Research." *Sociological Inquiry* 56 (1):2–29.

Cook, Karen S. 1982. "Network Structures from an Exchange Perspective." In Peter V. Marsden and Nan Lin (eds.), *Social Structure and Network Analysis.* Beverly Hills: Sage.

Cook, Karen S., Richard M. Emerson, Mary R. Gilmore, and Toshio Yamagishi. 1983. "The Distribution of Power in Exchange Networks: Theory and Experimental Results." *American Journal of Sociology.* 89:721–39.

Cook, Karen S., Mary R. Gillmore, and Toshio Yamagishi. 1986. "Point and Line Vulnerability as Bases for Predicting the Distribution.

Coser, Lewis A. 1956. *The Functions of Social Conflict.* New York: Free Press.

Coser, Rose Laub. 1989. "Reflections on Feminist Theory." In Ruth Wallace (ed.), *Feminism and Sociological Theory.* Newbury Park, CA: Sage.

Costner, Herbert L., and Robert Leik. 1963. "Deductions from Axiomatic Theory." *American Sociological Review* 28:819–35.

Curtis, Richard. 1986. "Household and Family Theory on Inequality." *American Sociological Review* 51:168–83.

Dahrendorf, Ralf. 1959. *Class and Class Conflict in Industrial Society.* Stanford: Stanford University Press.

Denzen, Norman. 1988. "Blue Velvet: Postmodern Contradictions." *Theory, Culture and Society* 5:461–73.

Dubin, Robert. 1969. *Theory Building.* New York: Free Press.

————. 1978. *Theory Building.* Rev. ed. New York: Free Press.

Durkheim, Emile. 1893 [1947]. *The Division of Labor in Society.* New York: Free Press.

————. 1895 [1938]. *The Rules of the Sociological Method.* New York: Free Press.

Elster, Jon. 1985. *Making Sense of Marx.* Cambridge: Cambridge University Press.

Elster John. 1989. Nuts and bolts for the Social Sciences. Cambridge University Press, NY.

Emerson, Richard M. 1972. "Exchange Theory, Part I: A Psychological Basis for Exchange. Part II. Exchange Relations and Network Structures." In Joseph Berger, Morris Zelditch Jr., and Bo Anderson (eds.), *Sociological Theories in Progress.* New York: Houghton Mifflin.

Epstein, Cynthia Fuchs. 1988. *Deceptive Distinctions: Sex, Gender, and the Social Order.* New Haven: Yale University Press.

Esping-Andersen, Gosta. 1990. *The Three Origins of the Welfare State.* Cambridge Polity Press.

Etzioni, Amitai. 1988. *The Moral Dimension: Towards a New Economics.* New York: Free Press.

Fararo, Thomas J. 1989 "The Meaning of General Theoretical Sociology: tradition and formalization" Cambridge University Press, Cambridge, NY.

Fararo, Thomas J. 1989. "The Spirit of Unification in Sociological Theory." *Sociological Theory* 7:175–90.

Fararo, Thomas and John Skvoretz 1984 "Institutions as Production Systems" *Journal of Mathematical Sociology* vol. 10:117–181.

Farganis, Sandra. 1986. "Social Theory and Feminist Theory: The Need for Dialogue." *Sociological Inquiry* 56 (1):50–68.

Freese, Lee (ed.). 1980a. *Theoretical Methods in Sociology.* Pittsburgh: University of Pittsburgh Press.

————. 1980b. "Formal Theorizing." *Annual Review of Sociology* 6:187–212.

Fuchs, Stephan 1992 *The Professional Quest for Truth: A Social Theory of Science and Knowledge* Albany, NY: SUNY Press.

Fuchs, Stephan, and Jonathan H. Turner. 1986. "What Makes a Science 'Mature'? Organizational Control in Scientific Production." *Sociological Theory* 4:143–50.

Gender, Family, and Economy: The Triple Overlap 1991 (ed) Lesser, Blumberg

Gibbs, Jack. 1972. *Sociological Theory Construction*. Hinsdale, IL: Dryden Press.

————. 1982. "Evidence of Causation." *Current Perspectives in Social Theory* 3:93–127.

————. 1989. *Control: Sociology's Central Notion*. Urbana, IL: University of Illinois Press.

————. 1990. "The Notion of a Theory in Sociology." *National Journal of Sociology* 4:1–30.

Giddens, Anthony. 1984. *The Construction of Society: Outline of the Theory of Structuration*. Berkeley, CA: University of California Press.

Giddings, Franklin. 1896. *The Principles of Sociology*. New York: Macmillan.

Gouldner, Alvin W. 1970. *The Coming Crisis of Western Sociology*. New York: Basic Books.

Gordon, Robert A. 1968. "Issues in Multiple Regression." *American Journal of Sociology* 73:592–616.

Gross, Llewellyn, (ed.). 1959. *Symposium on Sociological Theory*. New York: Harper and Row.

Hage, Jerald D. 1965. "An Axiomatic Theory of Organizations." *Administrative Science Quarterly*.

————. 1972. *Techniques and Problems of Theory Construction in Sociology.* New York: Wiley.

————. 1974. *Communication and Organizational Control: A Cybernetic Perspective in a Health and Welfare Setting.* New York: Wiley-Interscience.

————. 1980. *Theories of Organizations: Form, Process and Transformation.* New York: Wiley-Interscience.

————. 1989. "The Sociology of Traditional Economic Problems: Product Markets and Labor Markets." *Work and Occupations* 16 (4):416-45.

————. 1990. "Organizational Theory and the Problem of the Shift in the Phillips Curve." *Journal of Behavioral Economics* 19 (3):285–304.

Hage, Jerald, and Gerald Marwell. "Toward the Development of an Empirically Based Theory of Role Relationships." *Socimetry,* 200–212.

Hage Jerald, and Barbara Meeker. 1988. *Social Causality* London: Unwin Hyman.

Hage, Jerald, Robert Hanneman, and Edward Gargan. 1989. *State Responsiveness and State Activisim.* London: Hyman Unwin.

Hage, Jerald, and Charles Powers. 1992. *Post-Industrial Lives: Roles and Relationship in the 21st Century.* Newbury Park, CA: Sage.

Halfpenny, Peter. 1982. *Positivism and Sociology.* London: George Allen and Unwin.

Hannan, Michael, and John Freeman. 1989. *Population Ecology.* Cambridge, MA: Harvard University Press.

Hechter, Michael. 1987. *Principles of Group Solidarity.* Berkeley, CA: University of California Press.

Hechter, Michael. 1987. Principles of Group Solidarity, University of California Press: Berkeley.

Hodson, Randy, and Kaufman. 1982. "Economic Dualism: A Critical Review *American Sociological Review* 47:727–39.

Hollingsworth, J. Rogers. 1986. *A Political Economy of Medicine: Great Britain and the United States.* Baltimore: Johns Hopkins University Press.

Homans, George. 1950. *The Human Group.* New York: Harcourt and Brace.

————. 1961. *The Elements of Social Behavior.* New York: Harcourt, Brace and Jovanovich.

Huber, Joan. 1988. "A Theory of Family, Economy, and Gender." *Journal of Family Issues* 9 (1):9–26.

Kahn, Robert, et al. 1964. *Organizational Stress.* New York: Wiley.

Kahneman, D., and A. Tversky. 1979. "Prospect Theory: An Analysis of Decision under Risk." *Econometrica* 47:263–91.

Kahneman, Daniel and Amos Tversky 1979 "Prospect Theory: An Analysis of Decision Under Risk" *Econometrica* 47(2) 263–91.

Kalleberg, Arnold, and Iving Berg. 1988. "Work Structure and Markets: An Analytical Framework." In G. Farkasund and P. England and (eds.), *Industries, Firms, and Jales: Sociological and Economic Approaches.* New York: Plenum.

Kanter, Rosabeth Moss. 1977. *Men and Women of the Corporation.* New York: Basic Books.

Kasper, Anne. 1986. "Consciousness Re-Evaluated: Interpretive Theory and Feminist Scholarship." *Sociological Inquiry* 56:30–49.

Korpi, Walter. 1989. "Power, Politics, and State Autonomy in the Development of Social Citizenship." *American Sociological Review* 54: 1309–28.

Kuhn, Thomas S. 1970. *The Structure of Scientific Revolutions.* 2nd ed. Chicago: University of Chicago Press.

Lakatos, Imre. 1970. "Falsification and the Methodology of Scientific Research Programs." In Imre Lakatos and Alan Musgrave (eds.), *Criticism and the Growth of Knowledge.* Cambridge: Cambridge University Press.

————. 1978. *The Methodology of Scientific Research Programmes.* Cambridge: Cambridge University Press.

Laudan, Larry. 1977. *Progress and Its Problems.* Berkeley, CA: University of California Press.

————. 1982. *Science and Values.* Berkeley, CA: University of California Press.

Lawrence, Paul R., and Jay W. Lorsch. 1967. *Organization and Environment: Managing Differentiation and Integration.* Cambridge, MA: Harvard University Press.

Lee, Margaret, and Richard Ofshe. 1981. "The Impact of Behavioral Style and Status Characteristics on Social Influences: A Test of Two Competing Theories." *Social Psychology Quarterly* 44:73–82.

Lenski, Gerhard. 1988. "Rethinking Macrosociological Theory." *American Sociological Review* 53:163–71.

Long, Susan. 1980. "The Continuing Debate over the Use of Ratio Variables: Facts and Fiction." In Karl F. Schuessler (ed.), *Sociological Methodology, 1980.* San Francisco: Jossey-Bass.

Markovski, Barry, David Willer, and Travis Patton. 1988. "Power Relations in Exchange Networks." *American Sociological Review* 53: 220–36.

————. 1990. "Theory, Evidence and Intuition: Reply to Yamagishi and Cook." *American Sociological Review* 55:300–305.

Merton, Robert K. 1968. *Social Theory and Social Structure.* 3rd ed. New York: Free Press.

Merton, Robert, Leonard Broom, and Leonard Cottrell (eds.). 1959 *Sociology Today.* New York: Basic Books.

Meyer, John, and Brian Rowan. 1977. "Institutionalized Organizations: Formal Structure as Myth and Ceremony." *American Journal of Sociology* 83:340–63.

Mies, Marcia. 1983. "Towards a Methodology for Feminist Research." In Bowles and R. Klein (eds.), *Theories of Women's Studies*. Boston: Routledge and Kegan Paul.

Miller, Joanne, Carmi Schooler, Melvin Kohn, and Karen Miller. 1983. "Women and Work: The Psychological Effects of Occupational Conditions." In M. Kohn and S. Schooler (eds.), *Work and Personality: An Inquiry into the Impact of Social Stratification*. Norwood, NJ: Ablex.

Mills, C. Wright. 1959. *The Sociological Imagination*. New York: Oxford University Press.

Mullins, Nicholas C. 1971. *The Art of Theory*. New York: Harper and Row.

Myerson, R. B. 1977. "Graphs and Cooperation in Games." *Mathematics of Operations Research* 2:225–29.

O'Connor, James. 1973. *The Fiscal Crisis of the State*. New York: St. Martin's Press.

Orloff, Ann, and Theda Skocpol. 1984. "Why Not Equal Protection? *American Sociological Review* 49:726–50.

Owen, G. 1986. "Values of Graph Restricted Games." *SIAM* 7:210–20.

Park, Robert E., and Ernest W. Burgess. 1924. *Introduction to the Sciences of Sociology*. Chicago: University of Chicago Press.

Parsons, Talcott. 1951. *The Social System*. New York: Free Press.

Parsons, Talcott, and Edward Shils (eds.). 1951. *Toward a General Theory of Action*. Cambridge, MA: Harvard University Press.

Pawson, Ray. 1989. *A Measure for Measures: A Manifest for Empirical Sociology*. London: Routledge.

Pfeffer, Jeffrey. 1981. *Power in Organizations*. Pitman Press.

Pfeffer, Jeffrey, and Gerald R. Salancik. 1978. *The External Control of Organizations: A Resource Dependence Perspective*. New York, N.Y.: Harper and Row.

Popper, Karl R. 1959. *The Logic of Scientific Discovery.* New York: Basic Books.

Quadagno, Jill 1987 "Theories of the Welfare State" *Annual Review of Sociology,* vol. 13: Greenwich, CN: Annual Review, Inc. 109–28

Reynolds, Paul Davidson. 1971. *A Primer in Theory Construction.* Indianapolis: Bobbs-Merrill.

Richardson, Lewis F. 1960. *Arms and Insecurity.* Pittsburgh: Boxwood:

Risman, Barbara. 1987. "Intimate Relationships from a Microstructural Perspective: Men Who Mother." *Gender and Society* 1 (1):7–32.

Risman, Barbara, and Pepper Schwartz. 1989. "Being Gendered: A Microstructural View of Intimate Relationships." In B. Risman and P. Schwartz (eds.), *Gender in Intimate Relationships.* Belmont, CA: Wadsworth.

Ritzer, George. 1975. *Sociology: A Multiple Paradigm Science.* Boston: Allyn and Bacon.

———. 1990. "The Current Status of Sociological Theory: The New Syntheses." In George Ritzer (ed.), *Frontiers of Social Theory: The New Syntheses.* New York: Columbia University Press.

———. 1991. *Metatheorizing in Sociology.* Lexington, MA: D. C. Heath.

Scherer, F. M. 1980. *Industrial Market Structure and Economic Performance.* 2nd ed. Chicago: Rand McNally.

Schotter, Andrew 1981 *The Economic Theory of Institutions* Cambridge: Cambridge University Press.

Simon, H. 1957. *Models of Man.* New York: Wiley.

Smith, Dorothy E. 1974. "Women's Perspective as a Radical Critique of Sociology." *Sociological Inquiry* 44 (1):7–13.

———. 1979. "A Sociology for Women." In Sherman and Beck (eds.), *The Prism of Sex: Essays in the Sociology of Knowledge.* Madison: University of Wisconsin Press.

————. 1987. *The Everyday World as Problematic: A Feminist Sociology.* Boston: Northeastern University Press.

————. 1989. "Sociological Theory: Methods of Writing Patriarchy." In Ruth Wallace (ed.), *Feminism and Sociological Theory.* Newbury, CA: Sage.

Social Institutions: Their Emergence, Maintenance, and Effects 1990 (eds) Hechter Michael, Karl-Dieter and Reinhard Wippler.

Spencer, Herbert. 1874–1896. *The Principles of Sociology.* New York: Appleton.

Stacey, Judith, and Barrie Thorne. 1985. "The Missing Feminist Revolution in Sociology." *Social Problems* 32:301–16.

Stephens, John. 1979. *The Transition from Capitalism to Socialism.* Urbana, IL: University of Illinois Press.

Stinchcombe, Arthur L. 1989. *Theory Building in Sociology: Assessing Theoretical Cumulation.* Newbury Park, CA: Sage.

Turner, Jonathan H. 1989a. "The Disintegration of American Sociology." *Sociological Perspectives* 32:419–33.

Turner, Jonathan H. (ed.). 1989b. *Theory Building in Sociology: Assessing Theoretical Cumulation.* Newbury Park, CA: Sage.

Turner, Jonathan H., and Alexandra Maryanski. 1979. *Functionalism.* Menlo Park, CA: Benjamin-Cummings.

Turner, Stephen Park, and Jonathan H. Turner. 1990. *The Impossible Science: An Institutional Analysis of American Sociology.* Newbury Park, CA: Sage.

Ullmann-Margalit, E. 1977, *The Emergence of Norms,* Oxford, Clarendon Press.

Wagner, David G., and Joseph Berger. 1985. "Do Sociological Theories Grow?" *American Journal of Sociology.* 90:697–728.

Walker, Henry A., and Bernard P. Cohen. 1985. "Scope Statements: Imperatives for Evaluating Theory." *American Sociological Review* 50:288–301.

Ward, Lester. 1883. *Dynamic Sociology.* New York: D. Appleton.

Westcott, Marcia. 1979. "Feminist Criticism of the Social Sciences." *Harvard Educational Review* 49:422–30.

White, Harrison. 1981. "Where Do Markets Come From?" *American Journal of Sociology* 86:517–47.

Whitley, Richard. 1984. *The Intellectual and Social Organization of Science.* Oxford, England: Clarendon Press.

Wiley, Norbert. 1985. "The Current Inregegnim in American Sociology." *Social Research* 52:179–207.

Willer, David. 1967. *Scientific Sociology: Theory and Method.* Englewood Cliffs, NJ: Prentice Hall.

———. 1986. "Vulnerability and the Location of Power Positions." *American Journal of Sociology* 92:441–8.

———. 1987. *Theory and the Experimental Investigation of Social Structures.* New York: Gordon and Breach.

Williams, Robin M. Jr. 1947. *The Reduction of Intergroup Tensions.* New York: Social Science Research Council.

Williamson, Oliver. 1975. *Markets and Hierarchies: Analysis and Antitrust Implications.* New York: Free Press.

———. 1985. *The Economic Institutions of Capitalism: Firms, Markets, Relational Contracting.* New York: Free Press.

Yamagishi, Toshio, and Karen S. Cook. 1990. "Power Relations in Exchange Networks: A Comment on 'Network Exchange Theory'." *American Sociological Review* 55:297–300.

Zetterberg, Hans. 1965. *On Theory and Verification in Sociology.* 3rd ed. New York: Bedminster Press.

Subject Index

197

Name Index